Essential Guide to RenderMan® Shading Plugin Development

Understanding Bxdfs

Brad E. Hollister

Apress®

Essential Guide to RenderMan® Shading Plugin Development: Understanding Bxdfs

Brad E. Hollister
Carson, CA, USA

ISBN-13 (pbk): 978-1-4842-9391-1   ISBN-13 (electronic): 978-1-4842-9392-8
https://doi.org/10.1007/978-1-4842-9392-8

Managing Director, Apress Media LLC: Welmoed Spahr
Acquisitions Editor: Spandana Chatterjee
Development Editor: Spandana Chatterjee
Coordinating Editor: Mark Powers

Cover designed by eStudioCalamar

Cover image by @vikayatskinaon Freepik (www.freepik.com)

Distributed to the book trade worldwide by Apress Media, LLC, 1 New York Plaza, New York, NY 10004, U.S.A. Phone 1-800-SPRINGER, fax (201) 348-4505, e-mail orders-ny@springer-sbm.com, or visit www.springeronline.com. Apress Media, LLC is a California LLC and the sole member (owner) is Springer Science + Business Media Finance Inc (SSBM Finance Inc). SSBM Finance Inc is a **Delaware** corporation.

For information on translations, please e-mail booktranslations@springernature.com; for reprint, paperback, or audio rights, please e-mail bookpermissions@springernature.com.

Apress titles may be purchased in bulk for academic, corporate, or promotional use. eBook versions and licenses are also available for most titles. For more information, reference our Print and eBook Bulk Sales web page at http://www.apress.com/bulk-sales.

Any source code or other supplementary material referenced by the author in this book is available to readers on GitHub (https://github.com/Apress). For more detailed information, please visit http://www. apress.com/source-code.

Printed on acid-free paper

Table of Contents

About the Author

Brad E. Hollister holds a PhD from the University of California, Santa Cruz, in computer science. His research interests include scientific visualization, virtual reality for training, and computer graphics. He is also a GItHub Campus Advisor at the California State University, Dominguez Hills.

Dr. Hollister has authored the following books:

- *Core Blender Development* (Apress, 2021)
- *A Concise Introduction to Scientific Visualization* (Springer, 2022)

About the Technical Reviewer

Saty Raghavachary is an Associate Professor of CS Practice at USC. For the past 19 years, Saty has been teaching a mix of courses that span the entire CS curriculum from freshman to the graduate level: a new general education (GE) course on exploring computing, a new data science undergrad course, introductory programming (C++, Java, Python), advanced CG, front-end development, search engines, and databases.

Saty has 21 years of experience in the CG visual effects and animation industry. From 1993 to 1996, Saty was senior graphics software developer and software manager at MetroLight Studios, one of Hollywood's pioneering CG production studios that helped launch the amazing graphics industry that we have today. From 1996 to 2012, Saty was senior graphics software developer (11 years) and senior training specialist and training manager (5 years) at DreamWorks Animation, where he worked on (has movie credits for) 20 films such as the *Shrek* series, *Madagascar, Puss in Boots, How to Train Your Dragon*, etc. From 2012 to 2014, Saty was at Autodesk, the pioneering CG software company whose software (such as Maya) is used almost exclusively worldwide to create visual effects, animation, and game assets. Also, Saty has written two books on RenderMan, the industry-standard rendering software whose concepts originated at Pixar—he is the author of *Rendering for Beginners* and a co-author of *The RenderMan Shading Language Guide*, both of which are widely used in the graphics industry. Saty pursues artificial general intelligence (AGI) as a hobby and has recently published a couple of AGI-related papers at the annual BICA conferences. Saty obtained three MS degrees and a PhD at the Ohio State University and also did postdoctoral research there. He is a member of ACM, IEEE (Computer Society), ASEE, and American Mensa.

CHAPTER 1

Overview, Brief Contextual History, and Pixar's Non-Commercial RenderMan

The intent of this first chapter is to briefly outline RenderMan.[1] The book assumes readers already have some experience with rendering, or ancillary exposure to photo-realistic rendering. If not, the reader is directed to external information that describes rendering from the RenderMan perspective.

This chapter avoids using detailed mathematical formulas in the overview discussions of Monte Carlo integration and radiometry. The book treats these topics in more detail later, before describing their usage for plugins.

For context, we review RenderMan's history. We also look at the official Pixar documentation and installation procedures (especially under Ubuntu Linux, which is not officially supported).[2] There is additional discussion of RenderMan's variety of plugin types and a synopsis of bidirectional scattering distribution functions (BxDF).[3]

---

[1] At the time of this book's writing, RenderMan 24.4 was the current version.

[2] Unlike Red Hat Linux, which is supported by Pixar.

[3] The naming convention for the mathematical function is "BxDF," while for plugins, it is either "Bxdf plugin" or simply "Bxdf." This is consistent with the Pixar documentation and broader literature.

© Brad E. Hollister 2023
B. E. Hollister, *Essential Guide to RenderMan® Shading Plugin Development*,
https://doi.org/10.1007/978-1-4842-9392-8_1

Introduction to RenderMan

Today, RenderMan itself is a photo-realistic renderer[4] provided as prman, Pixar's own commercial and Non-Commercial RenderMan (NCR) reference implementation.

RenderMan takes as input a scene description and outputs a rendered 2D image. Included in the NCR tool distribution is a framebuffer program called it, as shown in Figure 1-1.

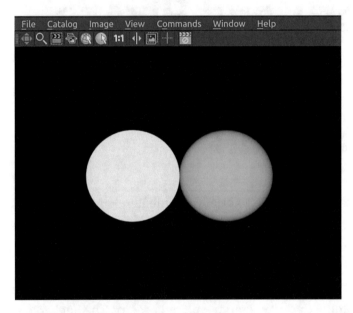

Figure 1-1. *The it framebuffer program, included in the NCR distribution*

There is, however, no native RenderMan tool for producing a scene description. A separate modeling program is tasked with this functionality. We will explore one such modeling "add-on" later (known as the official "RenderMan for Blender" tool[5]), which supports the RenderMan Interface Bytestream (RIB) in Chapter 9.

---

[4] Until RenderMan 20, "RenderMan" referred equally to its application programming interface (API) specification, as well as any particular implementation. Numerous implementations of its specification exist; one of the more prominent open source implementations is Aqsis (*https://github.com/aqsis/aqsis*).

[5] Official documentation can be found at *https://rmanwiki.pixar.com/display/RFB24/ RenderMan+24+for+Blender*. The open source for the add-on is hosted on GitHub: *https://github.com/prman-pixar/RenderManForBlender*

RenderMan is not a real-time renderer. Its API differs from those such as Vulkan, OpenGL, and Direct3D that enable the creation of real-time rendering engines. While RIB files can be updated and then rendered, and tiles are shown as the Monte Carlo path tracing rendering updates the image during the rendering process, no subsystem allows for dynamically changing the scene geometry for interactive image generation. Despite this, the programmable pipeline for real-time shaders, the OpenGL API in particular, was heavily influenced by the RenderMan specification.

The following are two seminal papers from Pixar's graphics library,[6] a set of freely available academic papers written by engineers and researchers from Pixar and affiliated institutions:

- Cook, Robert L., Loren Carpenter, and Edwin Catmull. "The Reyes image rendering architecture." *ACM SIGGRAPH Computer Graphics* 21.4 (1987): 95–102

- Christensen, Per, et al. "RenderMan: An advanced path-tracing architecture for movie rendering." *ACM Transactions on Graphics (TOG)* 37.3 (2018): 1–21

The former paper describes the original "Render Everything You Ever Saw" (REYES) architecture, which is what is called a "raster-based" algorithm. REYES was created for efficiency on computer workstations in the 1980s.

The latter paper describes the latest (as of RenderMan 21) architecture, as it is now a Monte Carlo path tracer. At the time of the original RenderMan, this was not a feasible option for creating feature-length animated movies, which was the primary intent of the original RenderMan software.

What Is Rendering?

Rendering is the process of taking a set of drawing primitives and applying a rendering algorithm that transforms the description of the scene elements using various parameters to produce a two-dimensional image. The rendering algorithm utilized may include elements of light simulation and geometric transformation, along with possibly primitive hierarchies forming objects. The surface of such objects will require a material definition describing mathematically how simulated light, if used, is scattered.

---

[6] *https://graphics.pixar.com/library/*

While RenderMan has altered its methodology for rendering, it has mostly kept its original scene description format (RIB).

Note   The switch from the REYES algorithm to Monte Carlo path tracing has considerably modified the ease with which small programs, called "shaders" (now plugins), add to the description of a scene.

The RenderMan Interface Specification

The RenderMan Interface Specification (RISpec) is an open standard outlined and documented in a single volume.[7] However, the current RISpec (2005) is not consistent with the most recent Photorealistic RenderMan (PRMan) renderer from Pixar. This dichotomy, especially regarding writing Bxdf plugins for surface shading, is the cornerstone of this book. The RISpec is for a version using the RenderMan Shading Language (RSL). Again, that standard is no longer supported by the latest Pixar RenderMan implementation.

Support for Monte Carlo path tracing has necessitated further updates to the RIB specification as well. Currently, no third-party renderer supports the feature set of Pixar's own `prman` as of version 21 or later.

A number of prior published references[8] address RSL and are consistent with RISpec v3.2.1. Prior knowledge and use of RenderMan implementations supporting RISpec v3.2.1 may be helpful for understanding the newer plugin architecture. Unfortunately, Pixar no longer offers a non-commercial version of `prman` supporting RSL, but Aqsis,[9] as mentioned, is available and supports RISpec v3.2.1. Familiarity with writing surface shaders in RSL is perhaps the best starting point.

---

[7] The RenderMan Standard v3.2.1 (Pixar) described the official specification and API as of 2005.

[8] Apodaca, Anthony A., Larry Gritz, and Ronen Barzel. "Advanced RenderMan: Creating CGI for motion pictures." Morgan Kaufmann, 2000.

Cortes, Don Rudy, and Saty Raghavachary. "The RenderMan Shading Language Guide." Course Technology Press, 2007.

Ebert, David S., et al. "Texturing & Modeling: A Procedural Approach." Morgan Kaufmann, 2003.

Raghavachary, Saty. "Rendering for Beginners: Image Synthesis Using RenderMan." Routledge, 2004.

Stephenson, Ian. "Essential RenderMan®." Springer Science & Business Media, 2007.

Upstill, Steve. "The RenderMan Companion. A Programmer's Guide to Realistic." *Computer* (1992).

[9] *www.aqsis.org/*

The Non-Commercial RenderMan

Free and open source versions of the latest RenderMan renderer—based on Monte Carlo path tracing as discussed by Christensen, Per, et al.[10]—are not (yet) available. Nevertheless, Pixar provides a free (but closed source) version called Non-Commercial RenderMan (or NCR for short). The first version of the NCR (RenderMan 20) was released in 2015.

Official Docs

Pixar maintains official RenderMan documentation.[11] Account registration is required to access official documentation. See Figure 1-2.

Note   The same registration is required to download the NCR.

---

[10] Christensen, Per, et al. "RenderMan: An advanced path-tracing architecture for movie rendering." *ACM Transactions on Graphics (TOG)* 37.3 (2018): 1–21.

[11] *https://renderman.pixar.com/*

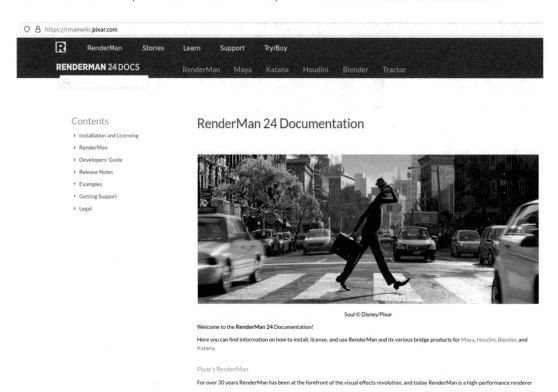

Figure 1-2. *Pixar's official documentation (RenderMan 24). The site is currently located at* `http://rmanwiki.pixar.com`*. Access is limited to those with registered accounts. Pixar still maintains a fully public wiki for RenderMan 20 (the first NCR version)*

Pixar's documentation includes information for both users and developers.[12] However, it is mainly intended for professional developers with prior experience in C++, RenderMan itself, and path tracing.

---

[12] At the time of this writing, Pixar continues to maintain a public wiki for RenderMan 20 (`https://renderman.pixar.com/resources/RenderMan_20/home.html`). This information is still quite useful, as the RenderMan 24 wiki is not as extensive in some concepts that were new when path tracing (i.e., the `Rix` Integration Subsystem, or RIS) was first introduced alongside REYES. Such topics as "presence," etc., are defined more thoroughly in the RenderMan 20 official documentation: `https://renderman.pixar.com/resources/RenderMan_20/bxdfRef.html#presence`. To better understand the context of Shader Plugins in relation to the older RenderMan Shading Language (RSL), see `https://renderman.pixar.com/resources/RenderMan_20/risDevGuide.html`

Installation directions are for supported platforms only. The rpm installation package for Red Hat Linux does work unaltered for other distributions, such as Ubuntu. Therefore, this chapter will address the issue.

Makefiles are provided for compilation of the plugins but are only guaranteed to work on supported Linux versions. C++ plugins are coupled to the underlying C++ standard libraries (OS dependent). Library interfaces are often compatible across OS platforms but still may need slight modifications or porting at times.

Official Example Plugins

Pixar provides a set of C++ plugins providing reference implementations of fundamental BxDFs. These are also part of the standard compiled plugins available in the RenderMan Pro Server. A useful addendum is the Doxygen HTML for the "RenderMan API" or Rix (RenderMan interface extension) API library. Plugins reside in a specific directory in the installation tree so that prman can locate and load them at runtime, as shown in Figure 1-3.

The Rix part of the RenderMan API, however, is not the "RenderMan Interface," which is the traditional C API (now with Python bindings) or the Ri library that allows modeling programs to output RenderMan Interface Bytestream (RIB) data. Bxdf plugins will reference the Rix API, rather than the Ri classes.

See the "Installing NCR on Linux Machines" section later in this chapter on how to obtain Pixar's plugin examples.

Figure 1-3. *Directory structure of the plugins distribution folder. PxrSimple.cxx and PxrDiffuse.cxx from the [examples directory]/plugins/bxdf/ subdirectory are good starter plugins to investigate. Notice that Pixar examples also provide scenes that showcase Bxdfs: [examples location]/scenes/bxdf/. The top-level directory, [examples directory]/utils/, is excluded here*

RenderMan's Evolution

To reiterate, one of the best sources of information for a historical perspective is Christensen et al.'s paper,[13] along with reading the seminal work by Robert L. Cook, Loren Carpenter, and Edwin Catmull.[14] For our purposes, we should realize that to write Bxdf plugins, a physically accurate form of rendering is used in RenderMan (different from the original REYES algorithm).

We will see later that a knowledge of probability and numerical integration, together with basic radiometry, is required. With REYES alone, this was not necessary.

Note However, for any single ray (a differential light contribution over a differential solid angle), the mathematics for a Bxdf plugin are very close or the same as an RSL lighting "kernel."

"Render Everything You Ever Saw"

As mentioned, REYES stands for "Render Everything You Ever Saw." The original depiction of this algorithm is shown in Figure 1-4, from Cook et al.

REYES was designed for efficiency. As such, it originally did not include global illumination (GI). That is, when shading "micropolygons" (roughly equivalent to differential surface areas), consideration was only given to direct light. All light contributions in the shading phase of the algorithm came either from lights or a constant ambient light term, used as a first-order approximation of global illumination. Diffuse interreflections (e.g., color bleeding by surfaces that scatter light in, more or less, equal directions from the surface) were not represented, unless baked into static geometry.

---

[13] Christensen, Per, et al. "Renderman: An advanced path-tracing architecture for movie rendering." *ACM Transactions on Graphics (TOG)* 37.3 (2018): 1–21.

[14] Cook, Robert L., Loren Carpenter, and Edwin Catmull. "The Reyes image rendering architecture." ACM SIGGRAPH Computer Graphics 21.4 (1987): 95–102.

```
Initialize the z buffer.
For each geometric primitive in the model,
        Read the primitive from the model file
        If the primitive can be bounded,
                Bound the primitive in eye space.
                If the primitive is completely outside of the hither-yon z range, cull it.
                If the primitive spans the ε plane and can be split,
                        Mark the primitive undiceable.
                Else
                        Convert the bounds to screen space.
                        If the bounds are completely outside the viewing frustum, cull the primitive.
        If the primitive can be diced,
                Dice the primitive into a grid of micropolygons.
                Compute normals and tangent vectors for the micropolygons in the grid.
                Shade the micropolygons in the grid.
                Break the grid into micropolygons.
                For each micropolygon,
                        Bound the micropolygon in eye space.
                        If the micropolygon is outside the hither-yon range, cull it.
                        Convert the micropolygon to screen space.
                        Bound the micropolygon in screen space.
                        For each sample point inside the screen space bound,
                                If the sample point is inside the micropolygon,
                                        Calculate the z of the micropolygon at the sample point by interpolation.
                                        If the z at the sample point is less than the z in the buffer,
                                                Replace the sample in the buffer with this sample.
        Else
                Split the primitive into other geometric primitives.
                Put the new primitives at the head of the unread portion of the model file.
Filter the visible sample hits to produce pixels.
Output the pixels.
```

Figure 1-4. *The REYES algorithm as depicted from Cook et al. (circa 1987).
REYES is a raster rendering algorithm. This type of rendering removes the need
for interpolation of shaded values over a polygon spanning more than one
pixel, where perspective-correct interpolation would be required. Even while
micropolygons are roughly similar to differential surface patches, they are first
shaded and then projected into screen space near the end of the algorithm. In
contrast, path tracing "samples" the scene by tracing differential beams of light
backward into the scene.*

RenderMan Shader Language

The final version of RenderMan supporting the RenderMan Shader Language (RSL) was version 20.[15] RSL was coupled to REYES in preceding versions of RenderMan prior to version 20. It was phased out along with REYES, but just before this RSL did integrate access to the RIS path tracer, for parts of the scene rendered using GI.[16]

What this means for RenderMan 24 users is that plugins now are dynamically linked with prman itself and must be compiled with a C++ compiler. Their object files are placed in the appropriate plugins directory where prman searches for library extensions. From a developer's point of view, mathematical functions (and other utilities, once RSL built-in functions) now have analogous implementations in the Rix API.[17]

RenderMan Bytestream

The RenderMan specification provides a command interface for the renderer, the RIB format as already mentioned, which communicates scene data and state settings. Figure 1-5 shows a simple example using the current Bxdf (implemented by plugins).

```
 2 Format 640 480 1
 3 Projection "perspective" "uniform float fov" [90]
 4
 5 Translate 0 0 3
 6 WorldBegin
 7 AttributeBegin
 8     Bxdf "PxrConstant" "name-for-shader-user-provided" "color emitColor" [1 1 0]
 9     Translate -1 0 0
10     Sphere 1 -1 1 360
11 AttributeEnd
12 AttributeBegin
13     Bxdf "PxrDiffuse" "disney1" "color diffuseColor" [0 1 1]
14     Translate 1 0 0
15     Sphere 1 -1 1 360
16 AttributeEnd
17 WorldEnd
```

Figure 1-5. *An example of the current RIB format using a Bxdf command. Here, we see both PxrConstant and PxrDiffuse (from Pixar), used for two sphere quadrics*

---

[15] *https://renderman.pixar.com/resources/RenderMan_20/shadingLanguage.html*

[16] Version info for RSL as published by Pixar in their RenderMan 20 documentations: *https://renderman.pixar.com/resources/RenderMan_20/whatsNewInRSL.html*

[17] *https://renderman.pixar.com/doxygen/rman24/index.html*

RenderMan has retained most of the RIB format syntax since its introduction.[18] This book does not discuss specifying geometry and scenes via RIB (nor the C or Python API, both of which output RIB). However, older references are still rather accurate in their descriptions of the RIB and C API.

C API

The first dedicated reference to the C API is Steve Upstill's classic, *The RenderMan Companion: A Programmer's Guide to Realistic Computer Graphics*.[19]

From Pixar's own current documentation:

> *The RenderMan Interface was proposed by Pixar in May, 1988, as a standard interface between modelers and high-quality renderers. To date, it is the only proposed rendering interface standard that includes provisions for all the features in a scene description required to synthesize photorealistic images.*
>
> *At the time of its introduction, the RenderMan Interface was defined in terms of a C language binding, a set of 96 C procedures that provides a complete rendering interface. Since then, a bytestream protocol has also been defined and incorporated into the interface specification. This protocol is known as the RenderMan Interface Bytestream (RIB), and it not only allows a scene description to be stored as an ASCII or binary coded file but also provides a means for transport over a network.*
>
> *—https://rmanwiki.pixar.com/pages/viewpage. action?pageId=61609200*

The C API is now more appropriately called the C++ API[20] and is part of the larger RenderMan API. RIB-related functions are prototyped in *ri.h* and prefaced with Ri, for example, RiWorldBegin() and RiWorldEnd(). See Figure 1-6.

---

[18] Initially, RenderMan only supported a C API interface.

[19] Upstill, Steve. "The RenderMan Companion: A Programmer's Guide to Realistic Computer Graphics" (1992).

[20] *https://renderman.pixar.com/doxygen/rman24/index.html*

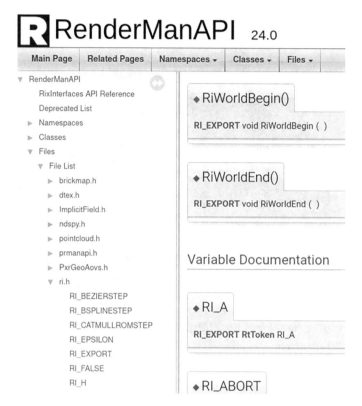

Figure 1-6. *The* `Ri` *documentation, a part of the official Pixar Doxygen hosted on Pixar's website. Note that the* `Ri` *part of the RenderMan API is presented together with the* `Rix`*, etc., interface portion of the API. We are concerned mostly with the* `Rix` *API related to Bxdf writing*

Python API

Pixar also provides Python bindings for the `Ri` interface. Figure 1-7 shows an example of an `Ri` Python script. The Python API can be seen as a convenience for producing RIB programmatically.

For performance-intensive procedural modeling, however, the C API is more appropriate. In this book, we discuss RIB and the programmatic ways of producing it for context.

```
1 #% setenv PYTHONPATH $RMANTREE/bin   # this is where prman.py lives
2 #% python
3 import prman
4 ri = prman.Ri() # create an instance of the RenderMan interface
5 rendertarget = "helloworld.rib"
6 ri.Begin(rendertarget)  # set rendertarget to ri.RENDER to render pixels
7 #ri.Display("helloworld.exr", "openexr", "rgba")
8 ri.Display('helloworld','framebuffer', 'rgb')
9 ri.Format(640,480,1)
10 ri.Projection(ri.PERSPECTIVE, {ri.FOV: 90}) # standard Ri tokens are available
11 ri.Translate(0,0,10)
12 ri.WorldBegin()
13 ri.Color([1., 0, 0])
14 ri.Translate(0, -1.5, 0)
15 ri.Rotate(-110, 1, 0, 0)
16 ri.Sphere(1, -1, 1, 360)
17 ri.WorldEnd()
18 ri.End()
19
20 import os
21 os.system('prman {0}'.format('helloworld.rib'))
```

Figure 1-7. *A Python RenderMan interface (Ri) script. Notice the similarity between the* prman *module's functions and the C++ RenderMan interface (Ri) C++. This script was written to invoke* prman

While it seems feasible there could be Python bindings for the Rix interface, as both Ri and Rix are part of the larger RenderMan API, this is not so. Recall that our Bxdf plugins are compiled to object files that are linked (dynamically) to prman. This is done for increased efficiency in the path tracing algorithm.

Overview of Monte Carlo Path Tracing

Since version 21, RenderMan has discontinued the REYES algorithm in favor of path tracing. With this change, RSL has been abandoned. Plugins are part of the programmable BxDF specification of a material and are responsible for calculating the probability density function (PDF) for each backward tracing ray.

Path tracing evolved from earlier ray tracing,[21] although it is considerably more general. There are two essential, and opposite, ways of rendering objects. The first is the raster-based methods that take geometric object descriptions and project them into screen space. This was shown in Figure 1-4 with REYES being an example. The second is the aforementioned method of tracing rays into the scene through the image plane.

Traditional ray tracing only handles specular light bounces through the scene. Monte Carlo path tracing, on the other hand, generates additional rays (in search of light contributions to the surface point being shaded). Thus, Monte Carlo path tracing handles not only specular interreflections but diffuse ones as well.

Further modifications to basic Monte Carlo path tracing are needed to support phenomena such as caustics. Bxdf plugins are locally aware of incident radiation and only need to calculate the probability density of each such differential ray.

A number of publications address the theoretical foundations of path tracing and therefore treat BRDF and related material on radiometry.[22] The key point for now is that as Bxdf plugin writers, we are concerned with the local differential (intrinsic) material properties and how to interface our plugins with RenderMan's Monte Carlo path tracing framework.

Note   There are plugin types that allow integration of differential rays to be implemented to specification. This book, however, is concerned with Bxdf plugins. While RSL gave access to a construct called an `illumination` loop, a parallel construct for the current RenderMan framework now lies outside of the Bxdf plugin (subsumed into Integrator plugins and the path tracing algorithm itself).

---

[21] Whitted, Turner. "An improved illumination model for shaded display." *Proceedings of the 6th annual conference on computer graphics and interactive techniques*, 1979.

[22] Cohen, Michael F., John R. Wallace, and Pat Hanrahan. *Radiosity and realistic image synthesis.* Morgan Kaufmann, 1993.
Pharr, Matt, Wenzel Jakob, and Greg Humphreys. *Physically based rendering: From theory to implementation.* Morgan Kaufmann, 2016.
Suffern, Kevin. *Ray Tracing from the Ground Up.* CRC Press, 2016.
Shirley, Peter, and R. Keith Morley. *Realistic ray tracing.* AK Peters, Ltd., 2008.
Jensen, Henrik Wann. *Realistic image synthesis using photon mapping.* Vol. 364. Natick: AK Peters, 2001.

Irradiance Integration

A necessary task of a physical description is to determine the amount of reflected radiance along a differential direction (from the differential surface location being shaded by a Bxdf). To do this, we must add the infinite differential incident light. This is called irradiance integration.

Usually, this is thought of as integration over a hemisphere, but as light can pass through materials, we eventually need to also consider integration over the unit sphere for translucent materials. However, let us start with opaque materials.

Your Bxdf plugins are not responsible for explicitly calculating incident light or irradiance summation. It is important to point out that we cannot take an infinite number of samples to do this directly, nor do we have a closed-form function that describes the light field. This is why we must eventually trace rays backward toward the original sources of light in a scene.

Numerical Approximation

At a differential surface patch, using a finite number of rays, we need to estimate their relative contributions to the integral. This leads us to a probabilistic numerical approximation called "Monte Carlo" integration.

Monte Carlo Integration

Monte Carlo methods are probabilistic techniques (using randomness) and therefore yield separate results every time they are applied. All runs, however, converge to the same method solution when performed with an infinite number of samples.

For our integration, if we know the exact contribution to the sum for any particular incident ray, then we must also (implicitly) know the integral. For a particular differential light source, its contribution would be its value divided by the integral we endeavor to estimate.

Instead, if we have a finite sum of randomly chosen differential rays, each weighted by their probability density function (PDF), which is defined to be their relative contribution to the entire integral (in this case, not only the irradiance but the radiance integral as a function of the total irradiance), then we can estimate numerically the integral in question.

By using the profile of the BRDF or close approximations, we can estimate the weights in the finite Monte Carlo sum for the true integral. It is best to sample incident light directions that have the most impact on the outgoing (reflected) light in the direction of the camera. This approach is called "importance sampling," as we will see later.

The more samples we take, the closer we approximate the actual integral. In practical terms, this usually amounts to a cosine-weighted distribution for the PDF, as we will see in later chapters. The RenderMan API provides utility functions for calculating these PDF values for a given ray so that we can pass this information to the integrator in the RenderMan framework.

Installing NCR on Linux Machines

The Non-Commercial RenderMan is free for download and use, assuming no content is produced for sale. A 120-day license can be renewed regularly on the Pixar forums. See Figure 1-8.

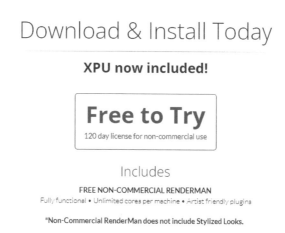

Figure 1-8. *The download site for Pixar's NCR. Note that you will need to renew your license every 120 days for the NCR*

You will want to make sure to download the examples provided by Pixar (Figure 1-9). When you run the installer, you should select to download both the "ProServer" and "Examples" by first checking the "Show All" option for all downloads and installations options available.

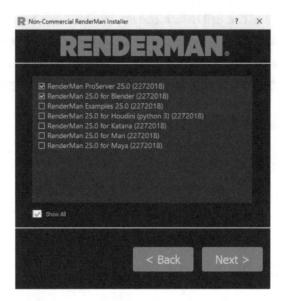

Figure 1-9.   *The RenderMan installer provides options for various items. For this book, you should install the ProServer and the Examples. Make sure to select the "Show All" check box for all download options. Version 25's installer dialog box is nearly identical to version 24, as shown here.*

Ubuntu Linux Installation

Pixar officially supports Red Hat Linux. Unfortunately, the installer for the Linux platform does not work "out of the box" with Debian/Ubuntu. For most users, this presents a problem but can be remedied by installing suitable versions of `libssl` and `libcrypto` for Ubuntu, as shown here:

1. Download the current RenderMan from Pixar.[23]

2. Create an account.

3. Download the installer (an `rpm` archive or "package" file for Linux).

4. If on Ubuntu, convert the `rpm` to a `deb` installer using `alien`. Then, install with `dpkg` as an administrator.[24]

---

[23] The NCR is available at *https://renderman.pixar.com/intro* (see also Figure 1-8).

[24] *https://help.ubuntu.com/community/RPM/AlienHowto*

5. The RenderMan installer program is unpacked in */opt/pixar/* (a system dir), which must then be run as an administrator.

6. On Ubuntu 20+, `libssl.so` and `libcrypto.so` are ahead of the version needed by the installer.[25]

7. To build `openssl` shared libraries (.so extensions), `cd` into the source directory.[26]

8. Type `./config` shared. Let autotools configure a Makefile for the build.

9. Then, type `sudo` make.

Note   Do not install the libraries as this may conflict with your systems installed openssl.

---

10. After the build is complete, copy `libssl.so.1.0.0` and `libcrypto.so.1.0.0` to */opt/pixar/RenderMan-Installer-ncr-24/ lib/3rdparty/Qt-5.6.1/lib* as `libssl.so` and `libcrypto.so`. For example:

    a. $ `sudo cp libssl.so.1.0.0 /opt/pixar/RenderMan -Installer-ncr-24/lib/3rdparty/Qt-5.6.1/lib/libssl.so`

    b. $ `sudo cp libcrypto.so.1.0.0 /opt/pixar/RenderMan -Installer-ncr-24/lib/3rdparty/Qt-5.6.1/lib/libcrypto.so`

11. *Be sure to install* `libtinfo5` *before running the installer.*

12. Then, run the installer from the *bin* directory.

13. Add the following to your `.bashrc`:

    a. `export PATH=$PATH:"/opt/pixar/RenderManProServer-24/bin"`

    b. `export RMANTREE="/opt/pixar/RenderManProServer-24"`

    c. `export PYTHONPATH=$PYTHONPATH:$RMANTREE/bin`

---

[25] *https://wiki.openssl.org/index.php/Libcrypto_API*

[26] Thus, you need to obtain the source for v1.0.0 and build locally. See *www.openssl.org/source/ old/* for openssl-1.0.0s.tar.gz.

Note   Make sure to type `source .bashrc` for the update to take effect. The ProServer version in your `.bashrc` script must match the version you installed. The Pixar examples will be downloaded to your default "downloads" directory, not */opt/pixar/*.

Other Types of RenderMan Plugins

There are a number of plugin types in RenderMan. We will be focusing on writing materials by implementing Bxdf plugins. However, some of the plugin types, such as Integrators and Lights, are coupled to Bxdf plugins, whereas others, such as Geometry plugins, are concerned with the surface geometry itself and not light scattering.

In RSL, one could write displacement shaders, light shaders, image shaders, volume shaders, and surface shaders. Some of these shader types are roughly equivalent to the newer plugins, and some less so. For instance, Geometry plugins are responsible for the same output as RSL displacement shaders, whereas surface shaders combine the duties of Patterns, BxDFs, and Integrators in the newer system.

Geometry

Geometry plugins allow for the alteration of scene geometry. This can occur at the level of vertices produced after a surface has been subdivided into micropolygons, where the plugin can displace the vertex being operated upon, or as entirely new geometry produced using procedural primitives.

Instead of specifying geometry in the RIB, it can be created during the rendering process. This is more efficient memory-wise and may therefore allow more detailed scenes. Indeed, very fine geometry such as fibers and fine hair strands may be modeled this way and treated not as a bulk (intrinsic) form.

Lights and Integrators

It is possible to implement Light and Integrator plugins, which both interact with Bxdf plugins through the `prman` framework. While RSL contained some of the functionality of Integrators within surface shaders, RenderMan's path tracing architecture is unable to make use of this and, instead, necessitates the writing of custom Integrators. Integrators give more control over path tracing, allowing variations on the path tracing algorithm.

In addition, custom lights can be implemented via Light plugins. Lights can be implemented using the `RixLight` interface (an abstract base class of the `Rix` RenderMan API). Such quantities as the light intensity, the shape of the light, and whether the light can be bidirectional can be controlled.[27]

Our Road Map

The purpose of this book is to cover local lighting behavior of intrinsic material properties by exploring how to write Bxdf plugins. The plan for the rest of this book is to

- Fill the gap between the sparse official documents aimed at professional C++ developers (with prior experience of physically based Monte Carlo path tracing) and those without such experience

- Enable technical artists to return to writing materials for RenderMan, as they were likely to do when RSL and REYES were used in prior versions

- Provide an accessible introduction to writing custom Bxdf plugins for students and hobbyists using the NCR

- Teach the underlying mathematics of Monte Carlo integration and PDFs needed to write Bxdf plugins in an intuitive way, thus lowering the barrier to entry for authoring custom material implementations

- Describe the physical models of well-known BxDFs visually

---

[27] This allows light rays to be traced both forward and backward through the scene for variations on the path tracing algorithm.

- • Outline the `Rix` RenderMan API and the related classes for accessing Render Context information and understanding the plugin execution model

What This Book Covers

This book covers most of the background needed to go from writing RSL surface shaders for materials to writing their equivalent Bxdf plugins. We will first cover some C++ topics so that those not familiar with C++ can also write Bxdfs.

Additionally, we discuss the practical mathematics of BxDFs and Monte Carlo integration, needed foundations for understanding the theoretical underpinnings of BxDF plugins.

After the introductory materials, we will proceed to investigate canonical BxDF written in the RenderMan Bxdf plugin format.

What This Book Does Not Cover

As already mentioned, we will not discuss how to author other RenderMan plugins. We will also not describe how to write `Ri` code to produce scenes, or scene geometry. We do not discuss how to write RenderMan add-ons or plugins for modeler programs.

Summary

In this chapter, we have provided a short overview of RenderMan. We discussed REYES and RSL, and the similarities to the recent versions of RenderMan. We also mentioned some of the basic requirements for writing Bxdf plugins, such as a knowledge of C++ and Monte Carlo integration. Additionally, we outlined the NCR and how to install it on Ubuntu Linux machines.

CHAPTER 2

What RenderMan Plugins Are Made Of: C++ Language and Shared Object Files

This chapter's goal is to introduce the reader to the programming language of shading plugins. The reader is shown how to build plugins for the RenderMan server and where plugins are loaded from.[1]

The C++ Language

Before we can delve into Bxdf plugin examples, we need to cover some preliminaries about the C++ language, as RenderMan shader plugins are written in C++ (and not like RSL,[2] which was its own distinct programming language).

---

[1] In Chapter 7, we will address how to link a prman process to plugins compiled with a debug option for symbol information.

[2] RSL has a C-like syntax. It contains built-in primitive types for vectors and vector operators. There is also a rich set of built-in functions; for example, there are ones for finding a reflection vector and obtaining a view forward surface normal. For C++ plugins, the RenderMan API now provides relevant equivalents of the earlier RSL.

© Brad E. Hollister 2023
B. E. Hollister, *Essential Guide to RenderMan® Shading Plugin Development*,
https://doi.org/10.1007/978-1-4842-9392-8_2

We will not teach C++ in its entirety here, as the language is too extensive and this book assumes familiarity with programming in C-like languages.[3] However, we do want to note the distinction between C++ and RSL and briefly discuss the language as a whole. This will make understanding how RenderMan uses plugins, and the development cycle of writing shader plugins, more understandable.

Note   Unlike RSL, C++ is a class-based object-oriented programming language. It is compiled. This means that its source files are translated to a hardware platform's machine-level instructions in order to be optimized for runtime performance. It has strong typing. Its current version is C++20 and is an ISO standard specification.

Reserved Words

You will find many of the reserved words in C++ familiar to other C-like programming languages. If you have done object-oriented programming before in languages like Java and Python, you will also see similarities between their class-based object-oriented paradigm.

While you should consult the aforementioned books dedicated to the C++ language, here is a truncated listing[4] of the most important reserved words. Reviewing these will provide an overview of the basic data types and statement constructs in the language:

- `auto`

- `bool`

- `break`

- `case`

---

[3] A number of works provide a thorough description of C++. Suggestions for further reading are as follows:

Meyers, Scott. *Effective modern C++: 42 specific ways to improve your use of C++ 11 and C++ 14.* O'Reilly Media, Inc., 2014.

Stroustrup, Bjarne. *The C++ programming language.* Pearson Education, 2013.

Stroustrup, Bjarne. *A Tour of C++, 3rd Edition.* Addison-Wesley Professional, 2022.

[4] A more extensive listing along with the versions of C++ where the reserved words were first introduced can be found at *https://en.cppreference.com/w/cpp/keyword*

- `catch`

- `char`

- `class`

- `const`

- `const_cast`

- `continue`

- `delete`

- `do`

- `double`

- `dynamic_cast`

- `else`

- `enum`

- `explicit`

- `export`

- `extern`

- `false`

- `float`

- `for`

- `friend`

- `goto`

- `if`

- `inline`

- `int`

- `long`

- `mutable`

- `namespace`

- `new`

- `operator`

- `private`

- `protected`

- `public`

- `reinterpret_cast`

- `return`

- `short`

- `signed`

- `sizeof`

- `static`

- `static_cast`

- `struct`

- `switch`

- `template`

- `this`

- `true`

- `typedef`

- `typeid`

- `typename`

- `union`

- `unsigned`

- `using`

- `virtual`

- `void`

- `volatile`

- `while`

The aforementioned reserved words, such as `bool`, `char`, `double`, `false`, `float`, `int`, `long`, `short`, `signed`, `true`, and `unsigned`, are each used to declare a variable's basic C++ data type, or the return type of a function. Note that in C++ 20, the number of built-in types is more extensive than this, but it is best to use the core set first while familiarizing yourself with the language. Also, the modifiers `signed` and `unsigned` are used in conjunction with the numerical types `int` and `short` to denote whether the data type supports negative quantities or not.

C++ supports pointers, which are slight abstractions of memory locations. Pointers are declared to point to variables of a particular type, such as `int` pointers or `float` pointers. Often, arrays are declared as pointers, if their sizes are to be determined at runtime and stored dynamically. Related reserve words for memory management are `auto`, `const`, `delete`, `new`, and `volatile`.

Control statements in C++ use the reserved words: `continue`, `do`, `else`, `for`, `if`, `return`, `switch`, and `while`. Additionally, there are statements that allow a programmer to specify user-defined compound or object-oriented data types such as `class`, `enum`, `struct`, and `union`.

Many of the remaining reserved words from our shortened list relate to data encapsulation and modifiers for access, such as `private`, `protected`, `public`, `friend`, `namespace`, `using`, `virtual`, etc. C++ has no particular reserved words for inheritance and uses a symbolic operator for this (i.e., the colon), unlike a language like Java.

Object-Oriented Programming

C++ supports a rich assortment of options for defining objects and the many object-oriented methodologies for working with objects. It allows multiple inheritance, abstract interfaces, "mix-in" classes, etc.

Understanding the object-oriented nature of C++ is very important, as the plugins you write will be derived from classes such as RixShadingPlugin and RixBxdfFactory. A firm grasp on object-oriented concepts is needed to understand the framework within which you will be implementing plugins. Consult the references on C++ if you do not yet have this familiarity.

Note   This is another area of departure from RSL, which did not support object orientation.

Compiling C++ Programs

For the examples in this book, we will be compiling under the g++ command from the GNU Compiler Collections, or gcc, C++ front end.[5]

We will develop our individual Bxdf plugins as (mostly) single C++ source files. However, incremental building via a build system, such as make, is still quite useful in order to develop multiple plugins for deployment.

In this context, "deployment" is the process of copying the Bxdf plugin compiled shared object files to the proper plugins directory. This is required so that the RenderMan ProServer (prman) can find them for use, which can be facilitated by batching multiple source file compilations together and only recompiling those plugin source files that have been altered since the last invocation of the build system.

Makefiles

A Makefile example is shown in Listing 2-1. The make utility[6] ingests a Makefile in order to invoke the system's C++ compiler and linker. Not only does make handle dependencies for compilation, but more complex steps in a build process can be included in the Makefile. Here, however, our Makefiles are kept to a minimum.

---

[5] A good reference to GCC, besides the official website (*https://gcc.gnu.org/*), is
Gough, Brian J., and Richard Stallman. An Introduction to GCC. Network Theory Limited, 2004.
[6] For more information on the make utility, see *www.gnu.org/software/make/* and *www.gnu.org/software/make/manual/*
Oram, Andrew, Steve Talbott, and Talbott Steve. *Managing Projects with make*. O'Reilly Media, Inc., 1991.

Listing 2-1. Makefile for building three cpp Bxdf plugins: BxdfDiffuse.
cpp, BxdfSpecular.cpp, and BxdfPlastic.cpp. The INCLUDES macro uses the
environment variable RMANTREE, the location of the RenderMan ProServer

```
CC = g++
CFLAGS = -std=c++14 -Wno-deprecated -fPIC -O3
INCLUDES = -I"$(RMANTREE)/include"
LD = $(CC) -shared
SOURCES=\
    BxdfDiffuse.cpp \
    BxdfSpecular.cpp \
    BxdfPlastic.cpp

OBJECTS = $(SOURCES:.cpp=.o)
DSO = $(SOURCES:.cpp=.so)
.SUFFIXES: .cpp .o .so

all:  $(OBJECTS) $(DSO)

.o.so: $(OBJECTS)
    $(LD) -o $@ $<

.cpp.o:
    $(CC) $(INCLUDES) $(CFLAGS) -o $@ -c $<

.PHONY: clean

clean:
    rm -f *.so *.o
```

Note   The .SUFFIXES line in Listing 2-1 specifies relevant file extensions for
the Makefile shown and default SUFFIX macros to perform. There is text
substitution for the definition of the DSO and OBJECTS macros, which replaces the
cpp extension for so.

Despite this example's relative simplicity, the following built-in macros may make it somewhat abstruse.

First, note that the top of the file contains macros that expand to their assignments on the left-hand side of the make utility's = operator. The $ operator preceding a macro enclosed in parentheses causes its expansion. For example, in the LD macro definition, we use the g++ GCC command as $(CC) evaluates to g++.

"Targets" refer to lines in a Makefile that contain commands to be executed by the system command utilities. They may have dependencies, and this is how incremental compilation and subsequent linking are achieved. Listing 2-1 not only contains a number of targets, but each target either uses the defined macros from the Makefile itself or one of the built-in ones such as $< and $@.

The build script produces shared object files (dynamically loaded and linked object files) as for the provided plugin source code. Because of the .SOURCES target, the suffix rules will be used. Thus, $< evaluates to a target's prerequisite (the portion preceding the colon on the rules line of the target) if the prerequisite has been modified after the most recent copy of the target. Similarly, $@ simply evaluates to the target in the command line, from the rules line. The macro substitutions in Listing 2-1 take place for .cpp source files, .o object files, and finally for the .so (or shared object) files. Thus, our dependency chain ultimately relies on the source files for each shared object plugin. We will talk more about shared object files soon.

The following targets are used in Listing 2-1:

- all

- .o.so

- .cpp.o

- .PHONY

- clean

.PHONY is used to ensure that the clean target is executed even if a file named clean exists, as the clean target does not have any prerequisites and would not run the command line if there is such a file.

Dynamic vs. Static Linking

There are two types of linking: dynamic and static. In RSL, there was no concern with this as the compiled shaders were not system-level object files. However, in the current Pixar RenderMan, plugins are compiled C++ code and as such must fit the conventions of linking with prman.

Shared Objects

As we saw in Listing 2-1, the output of our build process will be a corresponding .so (or .dll file on Windows, discussed more in Chapter 7) for each plugin .cpp file. RenderMan (more specifically prman) will access the source code definitions for the Bxdf from the .so file.

Plugins are loaded and linked at runtime and thus need to be compiled to a .so. The -shared g++ compiler option takes care of this for us (as shown in the LD macro from Listing 2-1).

Plugins Folder

Most applications, using a plugin architecture, have a standard location where the plugins must be placed. This can be configurable with some systems. While RenderMan allows the RMANTREE to be custom, the plugins folder is fixed relative to the root of the RenderMan ProServer installation directory.

Where the RenderMan Server Loads Plugin Binaries

prman will only use the shared object files placed in its */lib/plugins* folder. See Figure 2-1. On Linux, the default location is */opt/pixar/RenderManProServer-24.x/lib/plugins*.

Notice that a number of plugins are at this location by default and that the stock Pxr* Bxdfs are implemented as dynamically linked plugins themselves and are not part of the prman executable itself.

Figure 2-1. *The plugins folder is shown here in the default Linux RMANTREE location: /opt/pixar/RenderManProServer-24.x/lib/plugins. This is only a partial listing*

Summary

In this chapter, we saw that RenderMan requires Bxdf shader plugins to be implemented in C++. Another feature of C++ plugins is the optional use of an XML file, called the Args file.

While this is not required, Args files are used in order to register parameters with tools that incorporate RenderMan and need to allow setting the parameters for Bxdf plugins via the tool itself. If we are using a RIB file directly to interface with RenderMan, the Args file is not required.

CHAPTER 3

Radiometry and Bidirectional Scattering Functions

In order to write Bxdf plugins, it is necessary to understand the fundamentals of the "rendering equation." This chapter describes basic theory for writing Bxdf plugins. This chapter is concerned with basic radiometry, both the integral calculus used to describe its equations and its physical intrinsic quantities.

The information in this chapter is presented informally, but a serious attempt is required and will give a better contextual understanding of Bxdf plugins—so that basic conceptual mistakes will not be made, hopefully saving needed development time.

In older versions of RenderMan using only RSL, reflection models were intuitive, in that strict physical measurements were rarely considered precisely. However, when using physically based rendering, it is necessary to know the physical quantities that final pixel color values are calculated from.

The science of light transfer and scattering is called radiometry. There are a number of treatises where radiometry is the main topic.[1] Note that our treatment of radiometry is in service of writing local reflectance models (BxDFs) using mainly elementary analytical functions.

---

[1] The following are more extensive treatments, with intended applications to disciplines other than computer graphics.

Kirkpatrick, Sean J. "A primer on radiometry." *Dental Materials* 21.1 (2005): 21–26.

McCluney, William Ross. *Introduction to radiometry and photometry*. Artech House, 2014.

Radiometric Quantities

Radiometric theory reduces (i.e., models) the world by using differential quantities, or ratios of these differentials—called derivatives. Differentials can be intuited as infinitely small and of appropriate dimension for the domain in question but that retain the essential character of a material or element being analyzed, such as the radiant flux of an infinitely narrow (differential) light beam.[2]

Later, we'll consider each "point" location (more specifically, differential area) on a surface and describe how it is both a receiver of light energy and a potential reflector (or, more generally, scatterer) of that same energy.[3] First, though, we need to talk some about solid angles, which may perhaps be a new concept to you. "Solid angle" is used in many radiometric definitions.

Note   Ultimately, when using a computer to simulate physics, we resort to discrete (or finite) values. Additionally, we do not have a closed-form description of our "light field" (i.e., the amount of light energy and its direction present at each point in space at a given time) until we simulate light transport—despite knowing the locations of all emissive objects (lights). Surface scattering properties are often due to geometries but represented only by a differential surface area in our radiometric BxDF model(s).[4] In order to describe the smooth continuity of our surfaces, we use mathematical descriptions of scattering from radiometry. It is more efficient to describe light scattering properties as being intrinsic, or retained, in differential areas.

---

[2] This may be counterintuitive, as a differential ceases to practically have any dimension at all. However, it is the most general way to account for smooth transitions in space. A conceptual treatment of calculus, and its associated infinities, is provided in
Strogatz, Steven. *Infinite powers: how calculus reveals the secrets of the universe*. Eamon Dolan Books, 2019.

[3] This statement precludes emissive materials that are commonly called "lights."

[4] For example, anisotropic reflectance (where scattering is dependent on how the surface is rotated about its upward direction), such as brushed aluminum, occurs because of small, but still visible, grooves running in roughly the same direction. Another instance is that of hair fibers, where BxDFs model hair reflectance as a continuous intrinsic surface property.

Solid Angle

Consider how to measure angular extents in three dimensions. The two-dimensional version can help us to generalize. In Figure 3-1, we see on the left a two-dimensional definition of an angle "subtended" by another two-dimensional object, and on the right, an example of a three-dimensional "solid angle."

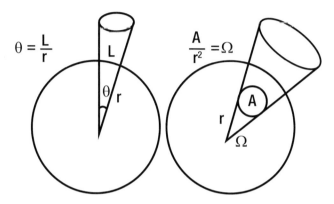

Figure 3-1. *The figure on the left is a depiction of an angle subtended (i.e., swept out or formed) at the center of a circle. We call this angle measurement θ, and it is the typical two-dimensional example. The angle is calculated by the arc length, L, divided by the radius, r, of the circle. On the right is a three-dimensional example. In this case, the angle subtended is called the "solid angle" and denoted by Ω. (Later, we'll see the differential solid angle is denoted as dω,[5] where it is a vector quantity representing both the direction of the differential solid angle and the solid angle itself as the vector's length.) Ω is equal to the finite projected area subtended, divided by the sphere's radius (also called r), on which the projected area is measured*

A solid angle is how we measure incident light on a surface's differential surface patch (intuitively, infinitely small squares in rectilinear coordinates). It is the range over which light rays from emissive or reflective sources arrive at a surface, measured from the perspective of that surface location. Units for solid angle are steradians, similar to the two-dimensional angle's radians. Steradians are abbreviated as *sr*.

---

[5] In this text, vector quantities are represented in bold type. Here, a vector is an n-tuple, that is, ordered set, of real numbers. The vector elements of the vectors depend on the dimensionality of the problem. This is generally three for spatial problems in computer graphics, although when transforming geometry, four-dimensional vectors are used.

Note   To simplify the use of solid angle measurements, we use the unit sphere, that is, the radius equal to one. Thus, the number of steradians in a solid angle is the projected area on the surface of the unit sphere (as dividing by 1^2 results in the same value as this area).

Differentials

We already talked briefly about differentials. In our radiometric view of light scattering, we'll use this concept repeatedly. For our purposes, we will not actually be calculating integrals within our Bxdf plugins. In fact, the samples are handled by prman. We only need to provide approximate contributions of each light sample as generated randomly from a distribution that we estimate. However, when speaking of radiometry, we need to consider the most general description.

Because our treatment is not at the level of advanced calculus,[6] we do not go into the details of limits or derivatives. It is a safe assumption to consider all quantities prefixed with a lowercase "d" as differential quantities, whose values are extremely small (approaching zero, but not entirely). For instance, a differential length in one dimension might be considered dx, where x is the canonical (standard) name assigned to lengths measured in Cartesian (rectilinear) coordinates.[7]

Differential quantities take measurements along the dimensions of the coordinate system used. If we are using rectilinear coordinates, then each differential is composed of linear dimensions. For example, a differential volume in rectilinear coordinates is an infinitely small (but not zero volume) cube.

---

[6] For more information on real analysis, see
Alcock, Lara. *How to think about analysis*. Oxford University Press, USA, 2014.

[7] You will also see radiometric differential quantities expressed with the partial differential symbol, that is, ∂, as in ∂x (for length) or ∂A (for area). This expresses that the variable quantity is dependent on more than one variable, in a broader (more general) model. For instance, see Jensen, Henrik Wann. *Realistic image synthesis using photon mapping*. Vol. 364. Natick: AK Peters, 2001, where partial differential notation for the radiometric quantities is used.

Radiant Energy

Now, we are ready to discuss the physical quantities relevant to a definition of light reflection in a physically based system. However, we will not be modeling light directly as electromagnetic oscillations, or quantum mechanically, as photons (although the intuitive notion of light particles may help us to visualize some of these notions as an element directed along light rays).

The first concept is energy, as this determines the brightness and color of our image's pixels. (It may help to refer to an introductory physics textbook here for a comprehensive review.[8])

A joule, J, is a basic unit of energy.[9] We use it to represent the amount of "radiant" energy, that is, the energy carried by, or synonymous with, light itself. *Radiant energy* is denoted as Q. A differential quantity of Q is denoted as dQ.

Radiant Flux

Flux is the quantification of flow. *Radiant flux* is measured in watts and used to quantify (measure) the amount of light energy that "flows," or transits, through a surface (real or imagined) per unit of time. The Watt is an SI unit equal to one Joule per second, i.e. $J \cdot s^{-1}$.

The differential quantity for radiant flux is denoted in terms of Q and time:

$$\frac{dQ}{dt}.$$

In subsequent definitions, we call this ratio Φ, as the ratio's value is not a differential quantity itself.

$\frac{dQ}{dt}$ is a derivative, so that the value of dQ depends upon dt. This ratio of differentials is particular to the moment when dt approaches zero, at some time t. $\frac{dQ}{dt}$ is considered "intrinsic." Scaling both the numerator and denominator proportionally results in the same quantity.

---

[8] Serway, Raymond A., and John W. Jewett. *Physics for scientists and engineers*. Cengage learning, 2018.

[9] We use the International System of Units (SI) in this book. However, we do not define the joule in terms of more basic units (see the aforementioned reference).

Note   The remaining radiometric quantities are composed of ratios of differential quantities. These ratios represent derivatives (of some underlying, although not necessarily known, function). When a definition uses an already-defined derivative, the subsequent quantity itself becomes a higher-order derivative (not simply a quotient of differentials as Φ may imply). This is why partial differentials are sometimes used to denote radiometric quantities.

Irradiance

Before we define radiance, we first define *irradiance*.[10] Prior to this discussion, in the definition for Φ, there was no mention of a surface through which energy is measured. See Figure 3-2.

Figure 3-2.   *Here, we have an area shown as a rectangle. Incident rays are measured as radiant energy arriving at the area. Note that this figure simplifies this greatly, and we see a finite area irradiated by only three differential light rays*

If we measure an area that receives radiant energy, we arrive at the definition of irradiance. When irradiance is defined in terms of finite quantities, we have $(\dfrac{\Delta Q}{\Delta t}) \div \Delta A$, or

$$\frac{\Delta Q}{\Delta t \Delta A},$$

---

[10] Irradiance has the same units and basic definition as a quantity called *radiant flux density*. However, radiant flux density applies to non-material (or imaginary) surfaces. In computer graphics, we are interested in the interaction of visible light with a material surface (or at least the ones simulated in our virtual scenes).

where ΔA is a finite area and Δt is some corresponding amount of time. ΔA may be a function of other parameters, but these are not relevant in the definition.

We, however, are interested in the more general definition of radiance using differential quantities, as it can be used over continuous space and time for calculations in radiometry. Irradiance can be defined in terms of differentials as

$$\frac{d^2 Q}{dt dA},$$

or, if we want, using partial differentials:

$$\frac{\partial^2 Q}{\partial t \partial A}.$$

This quantity is also known as E.

Partial differentials clarify that Q is a function of both t and A. If we use radiant flux to define radiance, then we dispense with the partial differential notation, as we hide the composite variables under Φ. Now, we have more succinctly

$$\frac{d\Phi}{dt}.$$

Note   It may seem as though we are overemphasizing differentials. These points are necessary, however, when we start using radiometric equations, such as for reflectance. It is also important to understand how ratios of differentials are properly calculated, that is, as derivatives.

The SI units for radiance are $(\frac{J}{s}) \div m^2$, which works out to be equivalent to $W \cdot m^{-2}$.

Radiance

We now discuss the concept of *radiance*. This is the quantity needed to calculate for each visible surface location (differential area) in our rendered scenes—that is, the amount of radiance reflected in the direction of the corresponding image pixel.

Radiance is defined similarly to irradiance, but now the "surface" is an imaginary (or conceptual) cross-sectional area along the direct path of light rays. The area is perpendicular to the center of this "cone" of light (Figure 3-3). Because radiance is defined in this way, the extent of this cone, that is, its solid angle, is significant. The amount of energy per time (flux) through this surface, per the corresponding solid angle, is termed radiance.

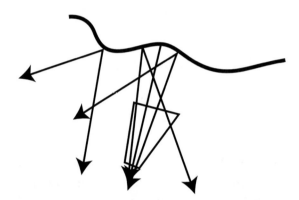

Figure 3-3. *This figure is cross-sectional for simplification. A scattering surface is drawn at the top of the diagram, and a solid angle cross section, measuring radiance, is at the center. A few representative rays are shown. Rays not converging to the "cone's" tip are not measured as contributing to radiance. Depending on the evaluated BxDFs, light scattering is distributed differently at each continuous point on the surface*

As we consider differential samples of light (synonymous with individual rays of light), we must also use differential quantities. Thus, the derivative for radiance (using partial differential terms) is

$$\frac{\partial^3 Q}{\partial t \partial A^{\perp} \partial \omega}.$$

This can be made more compact using a second-derivative definition involving radiant flux:

$$\frac{\partial^2 \Phi}{\partial A^{\perp} \partial \omega}.$$

Radiance is known as L.

The SI units for radiance are $W \cdot m^{-2} \cdot sr^{-1}$. Recall that sr stands for steradians, our SI unit for solid angle.

Differential Solid Angle with Respect to Radiance

A differential light cone has a differential solid angle $d\omega$. To associate a direction with a differential light cone, $d\omega$ is considered a vector in the opposite direction of the cone's narrower end, with magnitude equal to its differential solid angle. See Figure 3-4.

The differential cross-sectional area of this light ray (or differential cone) is $dA^{\perp}$.[11] This can be measured anywhere along the length of the cone as the radiant flux drops with the square of the distance to the source. The differential perpendicular cross-sectional area decreases proportionally in total area with the square of this distance, maintaining a constant ratio of energy flux along the cone's axis.

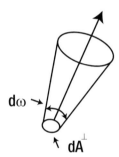

Figure 3-4. *The "light cone" opening in the direction of the incoming light ray (where the incoming light ray is opposite to the direction in the figure). The differential solid angle dω specifies the extent, or thickness, of the bundle of light rays all converging at the cone's tip. The polarity can be in either direction, as scattering functions are bidirectional. When measuring radiance, the solid angle is from the perspective of the measurement, not the radiant source[12]*

---

[11] You may be asking yourself where along this solid angle is $dA^{\perp}$. It turns out that is not important, as the radiant energy changes proportionally with the square of the distance to a source. Therefore, all along the cone, the radiance is constant. The solid angle opens toward the incoming light, so $dA^{\perp}$ decreases the further from the light source the measurement is taken.

[12] The following reference uses a canonical detector as an analogy to the differential solid angle of the light ray(s) for the measurement of radiance.

Shirley, Peter, and R. Keith Morley. *Realistic ray tracing*. AK Peters, Ltd., 2008.

Jensen, Henrik Wann. *Realistic image synthesis using photon mapping*. Vol. 364. Natick: AK Peters, 2001.

Definition of the BxDF

BxDFs are at the core of plugins for local material definitions. The primary task is to define a model, given a single differential irradiance on a surface differential area. This analytical model determines what the scattered differential radiance is for a directional differential solid angle direction.

Mathematically, this can be summarized as the differential radiance over differential irradiance:

$$f\left(\omega_i,\omega_r\right) = \frac{dL\left(\omega_i,\omega_r\right)}{dE\left(\omega_i,\omega_r\right)},$$

where both dL and dE are functions of the incoming and outgoing directions.

Note   Both ω_i and ω_r are directions (incident and reflected), not solid angles. However, the result of the function is a dimensionless value per steradian, in units of sr^{-1}, as a result of dividing radiance (which is per unit steradian) by irradiance, which is independent of solid angle.

This is known as the *bidirectional reflectance distribution function* (BRDF, or BxDF, if we consider it to be part of the class of more general scattering functions).[13] It is called bidirectional because if we swap the incoming and outgoing rays, the output radiance value is the same. This property is called *reciprocity*. It allows us to trace rays either into the scene from the eye (as is done in path tracing) or forward, as light transport in nature, and with certain variations of path tracing called *bidirectional path tracing*.[14]

---

[13] A BRDF may have values of zero to infinity. This can seem counterintuitive. That is, the differential reflected radiance for a differential portion of irradiance may be more than one. An instance of this is a perfectly specular surface, where all incident light from a single direction is completely reflected.

[14] For more information on bidirectional path tracing and path tracing in general, see Pharr, Matt, Wenzel Jakob, and Greg Humphreys. *Physically based rendering: From theory to implementation*. Morgan Kaufmann, 2016.

Rendering Equation

The *rendering equation* is an equation that we solve (approximately, via numerical methods) when rendering images using lighting. It contains many terms and uses the radiometric quantities already discussed. A constituent part of the rendering equation is the BRDF.

We do not specify a coordinate system here. The purpose of this chapter is to provide an intuitive understanding of the radiometry involved with writing Bxdf plugins, but not solutions to the equations. We do that in the next chapter using Monte Carlo integration.

Note   We focus on non-emissive (reflective) surfaces in this book so that we may safely ignore an emissive term. Thus, in this book, we technically are discussing the *reflectance equation*, that is, the *rendering equation* without an emissive (light emitting) term.

Let us show our "rendering" equation for calculating local light reflection first and then discuss each of its constituent terms. $L(\omega_r)$ denotes the finite radiance reflected from a differential surface being considered:

$$L(\omega_r) = \int_{\Omega} f(\omega_i, \omega_r) \cos(\theta_i) L_i(\omega_i) d\omega_i.$$

Note   All directions and angle measurements are relative to this surface and its principal orthogonal directions (analogous to the directions "up," "right," and "left").

The Integral

The rendering equation, as shown, consists of an integral. The limits of integration are stated succinctly as Ω, to denote a finite solid angle. The extent of that domain is usually a hemisphere, as that encompasses all incident light on one side of a differential surface.

The integrand terms are evaluated for each direction and weighted by the differential solid angle $d\omega_i$, for each of the infinite directions about the hemisphere (Figure 3-5).

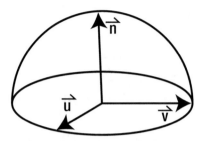

Figure 3-5. *The "unit" hemisphere about which we will integrate our rendering integral. The full extent of the hemisphere's solid angle is 2π. Note that this is because the radius is one and the surface area of a hemisphere is 2π, so that its surface area is also the solid angle for the entire hemisphere. The orthogonal angles of the differential surface area are also shown, which are **u**, **v**, and **n**, depicted as unit length vectors at right angles to each other*

BRDF Term

We already discussed the BRDF function in an earlier section. The BRDF is $f(\omega_i, \omega_r)$ and is evaluated for each incident light contribution at ω_r. The $d\omega_i$ term, when multiplied by the BRDF, cancels out, as we have radiance in the numerator which itself is per steradian.

Remember, each evaluation of the integrand over the hemisphere needs to result in differential contribution dL to the entire radiance L that is reflected from the differential surface for all incoming light.

Cosine Term

Finally, we have the cosine term. The angle θ_i is the angle between the incident light direction for a differential solid angle and the principal normal direction **n**. This is used to project the $dA^\perp$ of the incident radiance term L_i to the differential area's orientation described by its normal direction **n**. The effect is to dilute the incident radiance as a cosine distribution about the normal. Any incident angles greater than 90 have no contribution to the surface's irradiance.

Summary

This chapter informally covered basic information from radiometry that is required to understand how Bxdf plugins operate in the current RenderMan path tracing framework.

We also described the non-emissive rendering equation and its terms. It is the job of the Bxdf plugin author to define a Bxdf that is evaluated for each material over the relevant surfaces in a scene. This is a local problem of summing incident radiances and weighting them by the corresponding BRDF evaluated at the viewing angle.

As prman is a physically based renderer, you should be mindful of the physical quantities discussed in this chapter. For practice, you should perform dimensional analysis to verify that the integral results in the dimensions of radiance.

In subsequent chapters, we will address how this integral is evaluated numerically and what must be provided by the plugin writer for this to be done accurately by prman.

CHAPTER 4

Monte Carlo Integration and Global Integrators

Monte Carlo integration[1] is used to approximate the rendering equation by random sampling from a distribution that must be supplied by a Bxdf plugin. Thus, it is essential that Bxdf plugin authors understand what Monte Carlo integration is.[2]

Global integrators (themselves plugins) are introduced to provide context. However, an in-depth explanation on how to write Integrator plugins is beyond the scope of this book.

Numerical Integration

As we have seen in the last chapter, a Bxdf $f(\omega_i, \omega_r)$ describes a material's reflectance for a differential area. That is

$$L(\omega_r) = \int_\Omega f(\omega_i, \omega_r) \cos(\theta_i) L_i(\omega_i) d\omega_i.$$

Although we define $f(\omega_i, \omega_r)$ in Bxdf plugins, we do not know $L_i(\omega_i)$. We must sample $L_i(\omega_i)$ using path tracing. Therefore, we need a way to determine this integral numerically. In practical terms, we must provide the RenderMan framework required parameters to integrate for us.

---

[1] Kajiya, James T. "The rendering equation." *Proceedings of the 13th annual conference on computer graphics and interactive techniques*, 1986.

[2] The function that provides continuous relative likelihood is called the *probability density function* (PDF). It maps from each possible sample to its density of probability. We will keep our consideration of PDF simplified at first and assume a uniform or cosine-weighted distribution. The Rix utilities make hemispherical sampling from these distributions straightforward. See Chapter 8 for further mathematical description.

© Brad E. Hollister 2023
B. E. Hollister, *Essential Guide to RenderMan® Shading Plugin Development*,
https://doi.org/10.1007/978-1-4842-9392-8_4

Quadrature

A Riemann sum is a finite series. It is often used to help first define the concept of an integral. In a Riemann sum, the domain of an integral to be estimated is partitioned. Then, the sum of these partitions' areas (for functions of one independent variable) is added. See Figure 4-1.

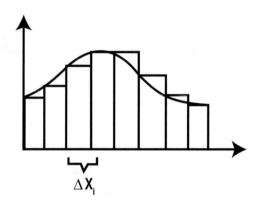

Figure 4-1. *A one-dimensional (single independent variable) function partitioned using a rectangular "quadrature." The definite integral of this function on an interval can be estimated by the sum of the areas of these partitions. Each partition is of width Δx*

The mathematical notation for a Riemann sum is

$$\sum_{i=1}^{n} f\left(x_i\right) \Delta x_i,$$

where the ith partition is $f(x_i)\Delta x_i$. There are n such elements. Each has a constant value (height) in the interval Δx_i.

A Riemann sum may be used with more than one dimension. Such a sum becomes untenable in higher dimensions (more than two). That is, each additional dimension requires proportionally the square of the number of samples from the lower dimension.[3]

---

[3] Variations on Riemann sums such as trapezoidal quadrature (where slices of the integral are piecewise linear approximations) can improve estimates. Quadrature numerical integration methods also require full knowledge of the integrand itself, which, for our light field, is not possible.

This is known as the "curse of dimensionality." This, and limited knowledge of an integrand, makes using Riemann sums (or other quadrature methods) unusable for solving our reflection integral.

Monte Carlo

"Monte Carlo" methods are wide ranging. However, we are concerned only with Monte Carlo for numerical integration. Broadly speaking, this type of numerical integration uses random sampling. It produces varying results for each estimation (i.e., for different sets of samples) but whose estimates converge to a solution with an increasing number of samples.

Note   Because of the included sampling functions, namely, `RixUniformDirectionalDistribution()` and `RixCosDirectionalDistribution()` from *RixShadingUtils.h*, we will use a cosine distribution for sampling. The rendering equation's integrand always contains a cosine term of the angle between the normal to the surface and a light ray. Therefore, rays closer to the normal have a larger effect on the integral, so sampling there is considered important and should be done more frequently than elsewhere.

Probability Density Functions

Since Monte Carlo integration is based on random sampling of the integrand, these random samples must be drawn from a function specifying their relative likelihood (i.e., probability density). Relative likelihood here equates to relative contribution to the integral. That is, the larger the integrand value for an input, the greater its likelihood should be for sampling. In our case, this is the likelihood of a light ray's contribution to the total reflected radiance (integral) at the differential surface area.

Note   Probability "density" is not the same thing as probability. Its range can be from zero to infinity. On the other hand, the probability of an event (i.e., a sample) is the fraction of this event out of all potential occurrences and can only range from zero to unity. For a continuum, as we have in physical space as modeled by real numbers, one discrete event has zero probability because there is an infinite number of divisions of the sample domain's measure. The differential probability for a given measure (sample space) is dp. Alone, this quantity approaches zero. Therefore, we must use this differential probability (dp) over a differential measure (dm) instead. This ratio, then, is probability "density." A PDF's value, for any particular discrete measure in the domain (sample or event), is its probability density (dp/dm).[4]

For our rendering equation, there are two-dimensional vector samples composed of the angle from the normal and the angle from the tangent. These angles are usually denoted as (ϕ, θ), with ϕ being the azimuth angle and θ, the angle to the surface normal. These are also the components for $d\omega$, the incoming light ray. This is the sample in our Monte Carlo estimate of the rendering equation integral.

To perform Monte Carlo integration, a PDF is needed. It should approximate the relative values of the unknown integrand. This PDF should be based on the known parts of our integrand. It is then used to determine samples from the integral's domain.

Usually, the details of determining a PDF and sampling from it are not required. But one needs to be aware of why the RenderMan framework requires a sample ray and its associated PDF value. In Chapter 8, we go over this process in more detail.

The Monte Carlo Estimator

The estimator for an integral using Monte Carlo is

$$\int_D f(x = m)\, dm \approx \frac{1}{N} \sum_{i=1}^{N} \frac{f(x_i)}{p(x_i)},$$

---

[4] Recall that ratios of differential quantities are derivatives (rates of change of one variable in terms of the other). Thus, a PDF's values are the derivative of another function that returns the accumulation of probability for a given range of measure. This other function is called the *cumulative distribution function* (or CDF) and ranges from zero to one in value. The total probability for all possible events must equal unity.

where *D* is the domain over which the integration takes place (and measured in *m*). Values of *x* are also measured by *m* but represent discrete samples in the domain.

x may be of any dimensionality (e.g., a vector or scalar). It is three-dimensional for the rendering equation. We use only two angle measurements to specify it, however, because we sample from the unit hemisphere. $p(x)$ is a PDF that approximates the distribution of values of the integrand. Each x_i is random, whose frequency of occurrence is that specified by the PDF. Again, $p(x)$ is usually taken from the largest known factor of the integrand and normalized to produce a PDF.

For a more accurate estimator (one requiring less rays and converging sooner), the BRDF portion of the integrand might be used together with the cosine term. This approach requires additional mathematical manipulation of the PDF.[5]

x_i occurs with the density distribution $p(x)$, and both $f(x_i)$ and $p(x_i)$ should have a common factor(s)—and thus similar shape. Large values of the integrand correspond to samples clustering around those values. As a consequence, we sample more of the larger values. As larger values of the integrand tend to be sampled more, they are weighted less, as shown in the estimator.

Error Determination

As mentioned, Monte Carlo methods produce different answers (estimates) for a given set of samples. Each estimate varies from the true value it is approximating. What is referred to as variance is the "error," or "deviation" of the estimator.[6]

For instance, this is best seen with interactive renderings. Variance manifests itself as the "noise," or abrupt differences in radiance between pixels that are close. As an interactive render continues, estimators get closer to the true value of the integrals. If you were to perform separate renderings of the same scene, you would see variations at any particular step in the renderings because of the random light samples. A "good" PDF reduces error.

---

[5] To aid in this approach, one may use symbolic mathematical packages such as MATLAB or Mathematica, as taking symbolic integrals is required. The nice aspect of using only the cosine term (known common factor) from the rendering equation's integrand is that it's only a function of the angle between the normal and the sample ray. If including parts of the BRDF, additional angles may be required.

[6] Or more accurately the squared difference of a particular estimator from the approximated integral.

Importance Sampling

If we use a suitable PDF for sampling and a sample chosen from this distribution, then our code will have performed "importance sampling." This is when we sample inputs to the integrand that produce the greatest contribution.

For us, this amounts to choosing rays that cause the largest contribution to the reflected radiance that reaches our camera. There are other types of sampling for Monte Carlo estimators, and you are encouraged to pursue this inquiry further.[7]

For all practical purposes, however, and in service of writing Bxdf plugins, the better our PDF is at matching the integrand's relative values for samples, the closer our estimators will be to the proper solution (i.e., low variance or "error"), and we will be doing this by sampling "more" important rays rather than "less" important ones—that is, rays that contribute less to the integral's total amount.

Overview of Integrator Plugins

While our focus is on Bxdf plugins, the machinery for integration is implemented within Integrator plugins. It is possible for users to create custom integrators, but Pixar already provides some. There are ones for forward path tracing and others that are not photorealistic or physically based. Note that we are talking about "global" camera ray integrators, not "volume" integrators, which are associated with particular Bxdf plugins. However, we do not discuss volume integrators in our introductory account of Bxdf plugins.

Official Integrators

Pixar provides the following integrators: PxrPathTracer, PxrVCM, PxrDirectLighting, PxrValidateBxdF, PxrDebugShadingContext, PxrDefault, PxrUnified, and PxrOcclusion. The first two are not included in Pixar's NCR RenderMan examples, but the remaining global integrators are. Therefore, it is possible to read their entire implementation.[8]

---

[7] See Dutre, Philip, Kavita Bala, and Philippe Bekaert. *Advanced global illumination*. AK Peters/CRC Press, 2018.

[8] In the future, Pixar may include more global integrators than those shown here.

You should consult the official Pixar documentation for a detailed treatment, both for parameter selection and implementation details. Integrators are mentioned here in the context of Monte Carlo integration to help inform you which integrators to use. Later in the book, there will be discussion on which global integrators are useful for development of Bxdf plugins. Chapter 7 covers setting up a development/debugging environment and reintroduction of appropriate integrators.

After we briefly sketch out primary global integrators and their uses, we describe some of the ways that integrators control Bxdf plugin instances. We only touch upon this, though, in terms of how it relates to general plugin architecture. To understand this interplay further, we need to talk more about the `Rix` API in Chapter 5.

PxrPathTracer

Path tracing is the method of recursively tracing differential solid angles of radiant energy or radiance backward from receiver (the camera's pixels) to scene objects, and ultimately the scene's light sources. The basic recursive path tracing algorithm is shown in Listing 4-1.

Listing 4-1. The simplified pseudocode path tracing algorithm.[9] Global integrators use `Rix`'s rendering services plus separate integrator and shading contexts for information such as normals and hit point lists. More is explained in Chapter 5. RenderMan global integrators, while implementing the bulk of the following, do not contain a Bxdf routine themselves

```
for each pixel {
    color = 0
    for each sample {
        pick ray from observer through random pixel position
        pick a random time and lens position for the ray
        color = color + trace(ray)
    }
    pixelcolor = color / number of samples
}
```

[9] From Jensen, Henrik Wann. *Realistic image synthesis using photon mapping.* Vol. 364. Natick: AK Peters, 2001. Shade points are collected into the appropriate shading context and passed to the Bxdf plugin as a collection. The Bxdf plugin must contain loops that handle each hit point.

```
trace(ray) {
    retrieve from integrator context's intersections with scene
    color = shade(points)
    return color
}

shade(points) {
    color = 0
    for each light source
        test visibility of random position on light source
        if visible
            color = color + direct illuminate via Bxdf
        color = color + trace(randomly reflected ray)
    return color
}
```

If you were to inspect the PxrPathTracer's source code,[10] you will see that it handles sending rays first from the camera (as part of the shading context for the hit points, which, as we will see, is an instance of RixShadingContext).

PxrPathTracer allows for diffuse and specular interreflections. At each shade point, however, the algorithm also samples direct lighting in order to converge sooner. The integrators take care of generating direct lighting rays, whereas for indirect lighting, the Bxdf plugins themselves generate rays (samples). As a Bxdf plugin author, your code needs to generate rays from a PDF that is associated with the integrand of the rendering equation, as stated earlier in this chapter.

Note   The official Pixar documentation has a number of renderings for comparison between Pixar's own integrator plugins.

PxrVCM

PxrVCM is a "bidirectional" path tracer. It not only uses direct and indirect backward-traced rays but also connects forward-traced rays from sources of light.

---

[10] PxrPathTracer source code is not provided in the sample integrator plugins from Pixar.

Note   For the Bxdf plugin examples in this book (Chapters 6 and 8), we use direct lighting to illustrate the reflectance properties of the df implementation.

If our purpose was to create fully rendered scenes and effects of global illumination, the PxrVCM would be a good choice for a global integrator—especially for scenes involving caustics. The same goes for the use of PxrPathTracer, already discussed, and PxrUnified.[11]

PxrUnified

Pixar uses this global integrator for its own films, utilizing both forward and bidirectional path tracing. Unfortunately, no source is provided for it in the NCR examples. It is similar to PxrVCM and will not be used explicitly in this book's Bxdf plugin examples.

PxrDirectLighting

PxrDirectLighting only computes direct lighting. You can inspect its source code for yourself. Try reading its code to better understand how global integrators are positioned within the data flow. Most significant for our purpose is that we can produce relatively fast renderings of simple scenes to illustrate developing and debugging Bxdf plugins.

The algorithm is simpler than a recursive path tracer like PxrPathTracer. Another exercise would be to extend this integrator to produce global illumination and then to compare scenes rendered with PxrPathTracer.

Integrators for Bxdf Development

While we will mostly create scenes using various light sources using PxrDirectLighting, PxrDefault provides a light source from the camera, thus not requiring explicit light instances and placement, simplifying scene construction for testing.

---

[11] Importance sampling is still relevant with direct lighting because modern RenderMan is a stochastic path tracer. Samples and their PDF values are required to be returned to the global integrator by the Bxdf plugin.

Integrators for Bxdf Debugging

`PxrValidateBxdf` and `PxrDebugShadingContext` will be used to illustrate debugging. These two integrators provide rendered feedback about inputs, or single-channel output, of a Bxdf plugin.[12]

How Integrators Call a Bxdf Plugin

Global integrators are instantiated for an image by the renderer. They then use the factory object of a Bxdf plugin to instance multiple Bxdf objects.

We will see later that there are two separate objects in Bxdf plugins. Most plugins share this separation of concerns. The "factory" aspect of a plugin is a specialized child class of `RixShadingPlugin`.

Analogy with the RSL `illuminance` Loop

If you come from an RSL background, you may see a parallel with a global integrator and the `illuminance` loop construct. Now, however, a Bxdf plugin does not have access to the lights themselves. RSL once combined patterns (procedural texturing), integration, and the Bxdf calculation into a single surface shading program.

Summary

In this chapter, we talked about the Monte Carlo estimator. We also saw that importance sampling is part of the numerical integration method and, when done properly, reduces error in the estimation of an integral. Lastly, we had an overview of Pixar's primary global integrators and how these interact with Bxdf plugins.

---

[12] Note that `PxrVisualizer` is a global integrator for understanding geometry but is less useful for debugging Bxdf plugins.

CHAPTER 5

The RenderMan (Rix) API

The purpose of this chapter is to describe the core header files (interfaces) and classes involved in writing Bxdf shader plugins. Topics include RixShadingContext, RixShadingPlugin, RixBxdf, and the utility functions (from *RixShadingUtils.h*). We draw parallels between the Rix API and built-in globals and utility functions from RSL.

It is important to realize that the Rix API is larger than we present here. Only a subset of its classes directly relate to writing Bxdf plugins. We will cover other parts of the API after this chapter, as they become relevant.

Classes for Bxdf Plugins

Common across all plugin types is RixShadingPlugin. Its definition is found in *RixShading.h*. RixShadingPlugin contains pure virtual functions[1] serving as an abstract base class (interface) for derived classes.

When writing Bxdf plugins, we must use RixBxdfFactory, which is defined in *RixBxdf.h* (and derived from RixShadingPlugin). RixBxdfFactory contains member functions (BeginScatter, EndScatter, etc.) that are pure virtual. These must be implemented by your Bxdf plugin implementation. See Figure 5-1.

---

[1] See Chapter 2 on C++ programming for more information on pure virtual member functions.

57

© Brad E. Hollister 2023
B. E. Hollister, *Essential Guide to RenderMan® Shading Plugin Development*,
https://doi.org/10.1007/978-1-4842-9392-8_5

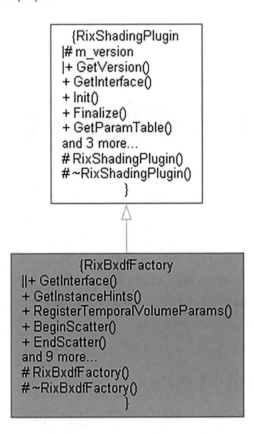

Figure 5-1. *RixBxdfFactory's inheritance hierarchy[2]*

In addition to a factory class (a child class of RixBxdfFactory), Bxdf plugins contain at least one more class definition derived from RixBxdf. RixBxdf is defined in *RixBxdf.h*.[3]

Another essential class for Bxdf plugin development is RixShadingContext. It provides the "built-in" variables for a set of shade points (i.e., a shading context) familiar from RSL. A shading context consists of the shading point locations, their surface normals, partial derivatives with respect to orthogonal surface directions (u and v), and more.

---

[2] UML generated by Graphviz Dot and Doxygen.

[3] Extensive comments are present in *RixBxdf.h*, which contains enumerations for various reflection and lobe types. It is important to read this "embedded" documentation thoroughly, either from Doxygen available from *https://renderman.pixar.com* or directly from the source, found in the Proserver installation location *RenderManProServer-24.x/include*.

Execution Model

For the code in this book, we will split our Bxdf plugin examples across two *cpp* files (with associated headers). The first will contain the "factory" class derived from `RixBxdfFactory`. The second will implement our child class derived from `RixBxdf`.

A factory will be called by a global integrator (usually `PxrDirectLighting`, as discussed in Chapter 4, during development) via the factory's `CreateInstanceData()` member function.[4] Multiple shading contexts may be active at any given time in more than one thread.

The shade points associated with any given context are processed serially in loops in the class you write that derives from `RixBxdf` (this class will be responsible for the actual Bxdf implementation, including the cosine term for radiance-to-irradiance conversion at the shade point being illuminated). The resultant outgoing radiance is returned by an "output" parameter (a pointer) to the calling global integrator.

The factory must perform some common but required tasks. These include using a preallocated memory pool for instancing `RixBxdf` objects and storing parameters passed by the RIB file to the renderer via a parameter table field in an associated `RixShadingContext` instance. A shading context is passed to the factory by its `CreateInstanceData()` member function.

RixShadingPlugin

Your Bxdf plugins will implement a factory class derived from `RixShadingPlugin`. The pure virtual member functions in `RixShadingPlugin` that need to be implemented are as follows:

- `Init()`
- `GetParamTable()`
- `Finalize()`
- `Synchronize()`
- `CreateInstanceData()`

---

[4] Example Bxdf plugins exhibiting this organization are presented in Chapters 6 and 8.

- `GetInstanceHints()`

- `RegisterTemporalVolumeParams()`

- `BeginScatter()`

- `EndScatter()`

- `BeginOpacity()`

- `EndOpacity()`

- `BeginInterior()`

- `EndInterior()`

- `BeginSubsurface()`

- `EndSubsurface()`

- `GetIndexOfRefraction()`

`RixShadingPlugin::GetParamTable()` must be implemented to gather the parameters from the RIB being passed to your Bxdf plugin. This factory function creates the parameters available to the Bxdf in the form of a load-time static array of variables of type `RixSCParamInfo`.

"SC" stands for "shading context." A context will contain parameters from the RIB that are passed to your `RixBxdf` object for shading calculations.

`RixShadingPlugin::CreateInstanceData()` fills out a `struct` of type `RixShadingPlugin::InstanceData`. InstanceData's field, data, is a void pointer. `RixShadingPlugin::InstanceData` also contains a copy of the parameter table for the Bxdf, created in `RixShadingPlugin::GetParamTable()`.

Note   We are using `RixShadingPlugin`'s scope resolution to clarify the particular member function. Your derivation of `RixShadingPlugin` will be responsible for implementing this interface and will be tied to the `RixBxdf` derived class that you write for your Bxdf plugin.

To keep the Bxdf plugins in Chapter 6 minimal, we implement `BeginScatter()` and `EndScatter()`, but not those functions related to opacity. Additionally, `BeginInterior()`, `EndInterior()`, `BeginSubsurface()`, `EndSubsurface()`, and `GetIndexOfRefraction()` are not required for opaque Bxdf with full reflectance (i.e., no transmittance or absorption of light).

In addition to these member functions, you need to provide externally linked functions so that the renderer can instantiate the factory. This is platform specific. Therefore, the `Rix` API provides the macro `RIX_BXDFPLUGINCREATE`, which expands to the proper function signature for your platform. Within the macro's curly braces is the function body. It needs to return a new instance of the factory to the renderer.

RixShadingContext

The shading context is the list of points being shaded, their built-in variables such as normals, u and v coordinates, etc.—along with the values provided as RIB parameters created in `RixShadingPlugin::GetParamTable()`. A shading context is contained in the renderer's derived class instances of `RixShadingContext` (an abstract base class from the Rix API) and passed to your implementation's `BeginScatter()`.

`BeginScatter()` invokes the "placement" new operator to instance `RixBxdf` objects, removing the need to use the operating system's dynamic memory allocation. `BeginScatter()` uses the shading context passed by the global integrator and forwards it to a `RixBxdf` instance. More on this in Chapter 6. See Figure 5-2.

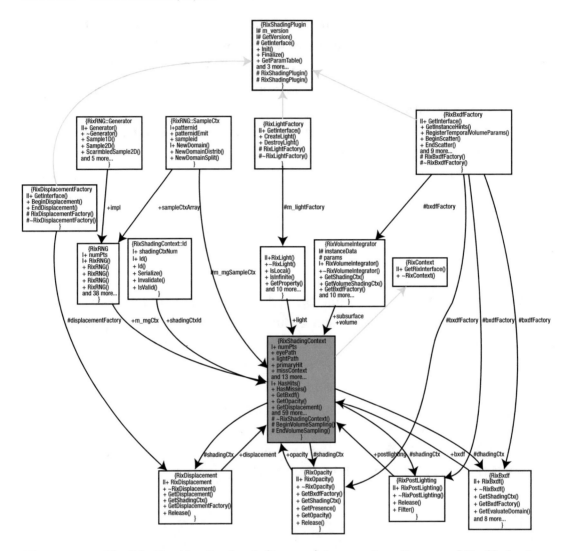

Figure 5-2. *The* `RixShadingContext` *(in gray) interaction diagram.[5] Bxdf plugin writers should take note of the* enums *and "getter" (accessor) member functions, for example,* `GetBuiltinVar()`, `GetParamVar()`, `EvalParam()`, *etc*

---

[5] UML generated by Graphviz Dot and Doxygen.

Similarity with RSL's "Predefined" Variables

It is best to refer to the official documentation for a complete listing and explication of the fields, predefined (built-in) variables, primitive variables, and parameter evaluations of RixShadingContext.[6] However, for those familiar with RSL, the shading context contains a familiar list of variables, described in RISpec v3.2[7] and in the RenderMan official documentation. Some of the most common variables are as follows:

- P

- dPdu

- dPdv

- Nn

- Ngn

- u

- v

- du

- dv

- Vn

- VLen

Note RixShadingContext instances contain an array of these built-in variables (called "predefined" in RSL literature) for each shade point in the context. There is a RixShadingContext::numPts quantity of them.

P is the position of the shade point in world coordinates. dPdu is the differential change of P with respect to a differential change in the surface direction u. dPdv is similarly the differential change of P with respect to a differential change in the surface direction v.

---

[6] See *https://rmanwiki.pixar.com/display/REN24/RixShadingContext* and *https://renderman.pixar.com/doxygen/rman24/RixShading_8h.html*

[7] The RenderMan v3.2 specification is included in the GitHub repository for this book. See Section 12, "Shader Execution Environment," and the "predefined surface shader variables" table.

Both dPdu and dPdv can be used to find the orthogonal tangent vectors to P, to produce a tangent space (orthonormal basis). These built-in variables will be used in anisotropic Bxdf.

Nn (similar to N from RSL) and Ngn (similar to Ng from RSL) are unit-length surface and geometric normals, respectively. The geometric normal is calculated from curved surface representations, while the Nn variable is determined by discrete finite differences between adjacent shade points.

u and v are the surface coordinates for P, and du and dv are the smallest finite differences between shade points in the shading context.[8]

Vn (as opposed to E from RSL[9]) and VLen (not included in RSL) are related to the "view" vectors in world coordinates. Vn is unit length, whereas VLen is the distance between the shade point and the camera.

We will be using each of these variables from the shading context in our Bxdf plugin implementations. As we progress to more complex Bxdf, including those that transmit and scatter light internally, we will broaden our coverage of the shading context.

Note   Recalling RSL, there is an L predefined variable (used in `illuminace` loops). However, L is defined not within the shading context for Bxdf plugins but by the plugin itself and returned to its associated global integrator. As stated in Chapter 4 (on Monte Carlo integration), we must generate our own light field sample ray first when the integrator calls the RixBxdf object in our Bxdf plugins, and then this new Ln variable is later passed to an evaluation member function (in the next section), that is, `RixBxdf::EvaluateSamples()` or `RixBxdf::EvaluateSampleAtIndex()`. For the direct lighting, the integrator generates Ln using the renderer's lighting services, as opposed to being retrieved from your Bxdf plugin's random sample Ln.

---

[8] We do not discuss s and t here, although they are also part of the shading context's built-in variables.

[9] RSL provides E (the eye position) instead.

RixBxdf

Global integrators instantiate `RixBxdf` objects, one per shading context. This happens when integrators call a Bxdf plugin's `RixBxdf::BeginScatter()` member function.

Recursive integrators will treat these calls to the factory as a closure, where individual Bxdf (holding state within individual `RixBxdf` instances) will not return until all light field samples have been calculated (or terminated) in order to provide an integral estimator in a given shading context. This, however, does not prevent additional cycles of light sampling.

Type definitions for `RixBxdf` are in *RixBxdf.h*. `RixBxdf`'s relationships to `RixBxdfFactory` and `RixShadingContext` are shown in Figure 5-3.

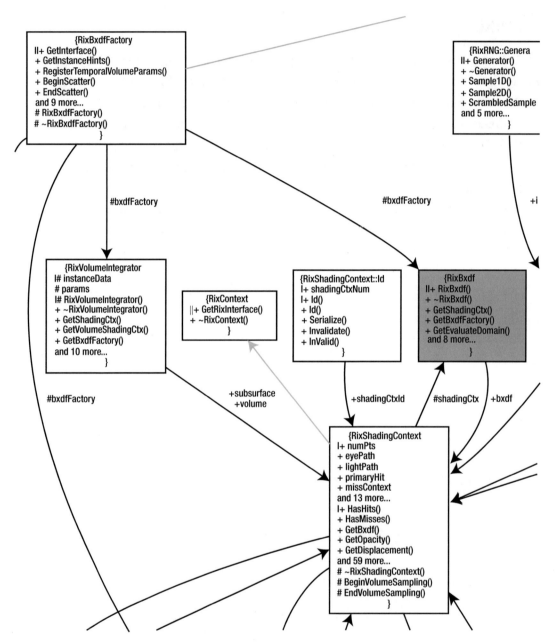

Figure 5-3. *The interaction diagram for the RixBxdf class (gray)[10]*

---

[10] Generated via Graphviz Dot and Doxygen.

For Bxdf implementations, we will need to implement the following pure virtual functions from `RixBxdf` (for opaque scattering materials):[11]

- `RixBxdf::EmitLocal()`

- `RixBxdf::GenerateSample()`

- `RixBxdf::EvaluateSample()`

- `RixBxdf::EvaluateSamplesAtIndex()`

`RixBxdf::EmitLocal()` is used for light emission. `RixBxdf::GenerateSample()` is where the `RixBxdf` definition, for a particular Bxdf plugin, returns a light field sample. It is called by the global integrator when needed after the integrator calls `RixShadingPlugin::BeginScatter()`.

`RixBxdf::EvaluateSample()` is overridden to implement the Bxdf itself. It is used to compute the rendering integral estimator's value for a single light sample per shade point in the shading context.

`RixBxdf::EvaluateSamplesAtIndex()`, on the other hand, is called for a single shade point. An array of light field samples are added to the integral estimator.

The global integrator determines whether to call `RixBxdf::EvaluateSample()` or `RixBxdf::EvaluateSamplesAtIndex()` for shade points and depends on both the integrator and the integrator's RIB parameters (i.e., number of light samples, etc.).

Shading Utilities

In addition to the predefined variables mentioned, the `Rix` API also provides utilities, much like the built-in functions in RSL. However, these are expanded upon in the `Rix` API, for example, those for calculating a lighting vector from a particular distribution. Most of these functions are inlined (using the `Rix` API's `PRMAN_INLINE` macro). The utility functions are defined in *RixShadingUtils.h*.[12]

---

[11] There are remaining virtual member functions as well, such as `RixBxdf::GetAggregateLobe Traits()`, that we will discuss directly in our example plugins for Chapters 6 and 8. The primary concern here is knowing which functions in the API are used regularly.

[12] Many of the utilities from *RixShadingUtils.h* operate on data from `RixShadingContext`. One could speculate that these utility functions might have been member functions of `RixShadingContext` instead. However, their usage has a broader scope, for example, `RixMin()` and `RixClamp()`.

Frequently Used "Built-In" Utilities

Some of the most useful functions in *RixShadingUtils.h* that compute vector quantities are as follows:

- `RixReflect()`
- `RixGetForwardFacingNormal()`
- `RixUniformDirectionalDistribution()`
- `RixCosDirectionalDistribution()`

`RixReflect()` and `RixGetForwardFacingNormal()` have direct analogous functions in RSL, that is, `reflect()` and `faceforward()`. `RixUniformDirectionalDistribution()` and `RixCosDirectionalDistribution()` are used for drawing vector samples from a hemisphere either uniformly or from a cosine distribution.[13]

Other utility functions will be discussed when encountered in our example plugins.

RiTypesHelper.h

Finally, you will notice that as we are using C++ (rather than RSL) to write Bxdf plugins, the `Rix` API needs to define mathematical objects such as vectors. These are found in *RiTypesHelper.h*. Some of the more common classes used in Bxdf calculations are as follows:

- `RtFloat3`
- `RtVector3`
- `RtColorRGB`
- `RtNormal3`
- `RtMatrix4x4`

Note   Each of these is defined in `pxrcore` and `typdef`'ed from its `Float3` type in *RiTypesHelper.h*. All of the expected vector operators are present as member functions.

---

[13] These are required for the light field samples in our Monte Carlo integrators.

Summary

In this chapter, we looked at the primary classes associated with writing Bxdf plugins. We saw that `RixShadingContext` is responsible for providing Bxdf plugins the points to be shaded and their surface characteristics.

There is an interplay between a plugin's derived `RixShadingPlugin` class (when instantiated, its factory object) and its derived `RixBxdf` class, responsible for handling the actual Bxdf shading calculations. Global integrators (discussed in Chapter 4) call a Bxdf plugin's factory object in order to instantiate multiple `RixBxdf` objects that concurrently execute to process a given shading context's shade points. We concluded this chapter by looking at the parallels between the built-in utility functions from RSL and the functions provided by the Rix API in *RixShadingUtils.h*.

Chapters 6 and 8 will cover example Bxdf plugins. More detail will be provided there, with further coverage of the `RixShadingPlugin` and `RixBxdf` interfaces.

CHAPTER 6

Canonical Scattering Regimes for Bxdf

This chapter describes canonical examples of isotropic and fully opaque material BRDFs:[1] emissive, diffuse, specular,[2] and plastic, as simplified Bxdf plugins. We outline writing a Bxdf plugin from scratch, building up piece by piece from information presented in Chapters 1, 2, and 5.

However, for the Bxdf in this chapter, the provided importance sampling uses a straightforward cosine distribution, via the `Rix` utilities for drawing rays from a cosine distribution—without mathematical justification for the calculated PDF values. We will explain forward and backward PDF calculations in Chapter 8. In this chapter, focus on becoming familiar with the structure of Bxdf plugins and the execution environment.[3]

In Chapter 7, we discuss using particular development and debugging techniques. You may want to read Chapter 7 first or stagger your reading of these two chapters.

---

[1] We use BRDF to refer to the function itself and Bxdf (plugin) to refer to a RenderMan implementation.

[2] Be aware that we do not discuss the geometry of the Phong specular component Bxdf (except to illustrate the notion of a multilayer BRDF and the `Rix` lobes). This is explained in introductory textbooks, for example: Peter Shirley, Michael Ashikhmin, and Steve Marschner. *Fundamentals of computer graphics*. AK Peters/CRC Press, 2009.

[3] This chapter does not explicitly set out the needed configurations, that is, from *${RMANTREE}/ RenderManProServer-24.x/etc/rendermn.ini, where RMANTREE is your server's installation directory*. When you are using a different directory than the default one for compiled plugins, `/standardrixpluginpath` must be assigned accordingly. This consideration is discussed in Chapter 7, where we talk more about setting up a development environment.

© Brad E. Hollister 2023
B. E. Hollister, *Essential Guide to RenderMan® Shading Plugin Development*,
https://doi.org/10.1007/978-1-4842-9392-8_6

Bxdf Plugin Code Organization

Each of the examples[4] in this chapter has plugins that implement two primary classes: a plugin-specific factory class and a RixBxdf-derived class. We talk about the factory code in earlier models (when our RixBxdf is relatively simple). In later models (especially in Chapter 8), we only discuss the factory when it becomes necessary. We use the RIB in Listing 6-1, with minor variations, for each of the examples in this chapter.

Listing 6-1. Simple RIB file used for examples. In this listing, we use the specular Bxdf from a later section in this chapter entitled "Specular Reflection Model." The chosen global integrator, light source, and Bxdf are in boldface

```
version 3.04
Display "simple_scene" "framebuffer" "rgba"
Projection "perspective" "float fov" [15]
Format 800 700 1

Integrator "PxrDirectLighting" "debug"

WorldBegin
  AttributeBegin # {
    Attribute "visibility" "int indirect" [0]

    AttributeBegin
      Transform [-0.427756 -0.624878 -15.1039 0
                 -6.3468 12.601 -0.34158 0
                 1.47654 0.74173 -0.0725036 0
                 48.0758 61.2751 -12.5641 1 ]
      Rotate 180 1 0 0
      Light "PxrDiskLight" "1" "float intensity" [150]
    AttributeEnd

  AttributeEnd

  Attribute "visibility" "int transmission" [0]
```

---

[4] See this chapter's source code.

```
AttributeBegin
  Bxdf "specular" "simple glossy shader"
        "color specularColor" [0.0 0.8 0.6] "float gloss" [200.0]
  Translate 0 0 8
  Sphere 0.8 -0.8 0.8 360

AttributeEnd

WorldEnd
```

To make learning the plugin's structure clear, we split our source code over at least four files: two *cpp* source files, one for the RixShadingPlugin child class and the other for the RixBxdf child, and then two header files, one for each *cpp* file. Our naming convention, for each Bxdf plugin, is as follows:

- *factory.h*

- *factory.cpp*

- *[model name].h*

- *[model name].cpp*

Emissive Model

While each of the examples in this chapter is relatively basic, a purely emissive model is the most simple.[5] Only a handful of member functions are defined nontrivially in both the RixShadingPlugin and RixBxdf classes. Regardless, our emissive Bxdf will help us to better understand the interplay between the renderer, the attached global integrator (in our case, PxrDirectLighting), the RixBxdf factory object, and the RixBxdf object itself.

---

[5] The examples in this chapter are renditions of canonical BRDF. The similarity between examples will be close even for our emissive Bxdf. In the set of example Bxdf plugins that Pixar distributes, this is close to PxrConstant. However, the official documentation does not explain (in direct terms) any of the official samples. We point out specifics here in earlier examples for this book.

Emissive Plugin Factory Class

RixBxdfFactory must be extended as it is an abstract base class (derived from RixShadingPlugin). We call our factory class SimpleEmissiveBxdfPlugin, and its implementation resides in *emissive.h* and *emissive.cpp*.

Much of its interface is unused for the emissive Bxdf, and for these member functions, null implementations are provided. These include the following:

- EndScatter()[6]

- BeginOpacity()

- EndOpacity()

- BeginInterior()

- EndInterior()

- BeginSubsurface()

- EndSubsurface()

- RegisterTemporalVolumeParams()

- GetIndexOfRefraction()

- Init()[7]

- Finalize()[8]

- Synchronize()[9]

That said, we first write non-null implementations for the factory creation and deletion functions to be used by the renderer. See Listing 6-2.

---

[6] Though not BeginScatter(), as will be discussed.

[7] SimpleEmissiveBxdfPlugin::Init()is used for any preliminary setup of the factory before the renderer makes calls to it. For our emissive plugin, we return a NULL value and do nothing.

[8] SimpleEmissiveBxdfPlugin::Finalize()is used for cleanup. It is not relevant for SimpleEmissiveBxdfPlugin.

[9] SimpleEmissiveBxdfPlugin::Synchronize()is also not used in this plugin. Synchronize() updates the factory to a new state of the renderer when needed. We will use this member function in subsequent plugins.

Listing 6-2. CreateRixBxdfFactory() and DestroyRixBxdfFactory() from factory.cpp

```
extern "C" PRMANEXPORT RixBxdfFactory * CreateRixBxdfFactory(const
char* hint)
{
    PIXAR_ARGUSED(hint);
    return new SimpleEmissiveBxdfPlugin();
}
extern "C" PRMANEXPORT void DestroyRixBxdfFactory(RixBxdfFactory * bxdf)
{
    delete (SimpleEmissiveBxdfPlugin*)bxdf;
}
```

Note   This function pair is platform specific and is best provided using the Rix
macros RIX_BXDFPLUGINCREATE and RIX_BXDFPLUGINDESTROY.

Here, the PRMANEXPORT macro provides platform-specific code substitution, but you
may also use RIX_BXDFPLUGINCREATE and RIX_BXDFPLUGINDESTROY macros, which will
expand to the entire function signature, only requiring the body of the function.

Create*() and Destroy*() functions must return an instance of the plugin's
particular factory implementation and on destruction also reclaim (delete) the
object. The PIXAR_ARGUSED macro is for all parameters that are not used by the actual
implementation to avoid compiler warnings.

On the factory, the remaining interface must be implemented for the following
member functions:

- SimpleEmissiveBxdfPlugin::GetParamTable()

- SimpleEmissiveBxdfPlugin::CreateInstanceData()

- SimpleEmissiveBxdfPlugin::GetInstanceHints()

- SimpleEmissiveBxdfPlugin::BeginScatter()

GetParamTable() is shown in Listing 6-3.[10] We hold the position of parameters in the table, for use in other functions of the factory object. RSL simply used the parameters of the surface shader function, but for a Bxdf plugin, there is a specific function called before any scattering is invoked by the global integrator on the factory object.

Listing 6-3. GetParamTable() defines the array (table) of RixSCParamInfo objects used by the renderer to determine the parameters that may be passed to the Bxdf from the RIB file

```
enum paramIds
{
    k_emissiveColor,
    k_numParams
};

...

RixSCParamInfo const*
SimpleEmissiveBxdfPlugin::GetParamTable()
{
    static RixSCParamInfo s_ptable[] =
    {
        RixSCParamInfo(RtUString("emissive_color"),
                       k_RixSCColor, k_RixSCScatterInput),
        RixSCParamInfo() // end of table
    };
    return &s_ptable[0];
}
```

CreateInstanceData() is shown in Listing 6-4. The implementation is sparse for our "emissive" example. In general, CreateInstanceData() is used for RenderMan's lightweight instancing mechanism/service. The data cached by this function can be used over the lifetime of the factory (plugin instance)—for use by the renderer and instances of the RixBxdf associated with the Bxdf plugin.

---

[10] The full example is found in *emissive.cpp* for this chapter's code.

Listing 6-4. CreateInstanceData() and GetInstanceData() for
SimpleEmissiveBxdfPlugin are shown as follows. As we do not need
to store data for this plugin instance, except the k_TriviallyOpaque
specifier, this implementation is sparse. The InstanceHints returned from
GetInstanceData() is a 64-bit bitfield set in the InstanceData "out" parameter in
CreateInstanceData()

```
void
SimpleEmissiveBxdfPlugin::CreateInstanceData(RixContext& ctx,
        RtUString const handle,
        RixParameterList const* plist,
        InstanceData* idata)
{
    PIXAR_ARGUSED(ctx);
    PIXAR_ARGUSED(handle);
    PIXAR_ARGUSED(plist);

    uint64_t req = k_TriviallyOpaque;

    idata->data = (void*)req;
    idata->datalen = 1;
    idata->freefunc = NULL;
    return;
}

...

int
SimpleEmissiveBxdfPlugin::GetInstanceHints(RtPointer
    instanceData) const
{
    uint64_t rawHints;
    memcpy(&rawHints, &instanceData, sizeof(uint64_t));
    InstanceHints hints =
                static_cast<InstanceHints>(rawHints);
    return hints;
}
```

BeginScatter() is responsible for instantiating the RixBxdf objects (more detail in the next section). Recall that BeginScatter() is called by the global integrator.

We need to copy the parameters from the parameter table as defined in SimpleEmissiveBxdfPlugin (from GetParamTable()) to each RixBxdf-derived object. This is done using a copy of the factory's member data—an array with numPts entries (number of shading points from the shading context). The array is passed to the RixBxdf constructor, in this case SimpleDiffuse(). See Listing 6-5.

Note   The factory must obtain, using EvalParam() from the RixShadingContext, an array the size of numPts, which is then copied into the RixBxdf. We set the default value of the emissive color, m_emissive_color, in the factory's constructor (not shown).[11]

Listing 6-5. BeginScatter() instantiates each related RixBxdf child object for a given shading context via calls by the global integrator. RixShadingContext:: EvalParam() returns an array of the parameter, whose length is the number of shading points in the shading context instance

```
RixBxdf* SimpleEmissiveBxdfPlugin::BeginScatter(RixShadingContext
 const* sCtx, RixBXLobeTraits const& lobesWanted,
 RixSCShadingMode sm, void* parentData,
 RtPointer instanceData)
{
    PIXAR_ARGUSED(sm);
    PIXAR_ARGUSED(instanceData);
    PIXAR_ARGUSED(parentData);

    RtColorRGB const* emissive;

    sCtx->EvalParam(k_emissiveColor, -1, &emissive,
      &m_emissive_color, true);
```

---

[11] Refer to *factory.cpp* from the emissive example of this chapter.

```
RixShadingContext::Allocator pool(sCtx);
void* mem = pool.AllocForBxdf< SimpleEmissive >(1);
SimpleDiffuse* eval = new (mem) SimpleEmissive(sCtx, this,
    lobesWanted, diff);

    return eval;
}
```

Emissive Plugin RixBxdf Class

The RixBxdf-derived class, SimpleEmissive,[12] implements the following interface member functions:

- SimpleEmissive()[13]

- SimpleEmissive::EmitLocal()

SimpleEmissive::EmitLocal() produces the final result for the surface point color. See Listing 6-6.

Listing 6-6. EmitLocal() from emissive.cpp

```
virtual bool EmitLocal(RtColorRGB* result)
{
    int nPts = shadingCtx->numPts;
    for (int i = 0; i < nPts; i++){
        result[i] = m_emissiveColor[i];
    }
    return true;
}
```

---

[12] Found in *emissive.cpp* and *emissive.h* for Chapter 6 code.

[13] The constructor sets the emissive color in an instance variable called m_emissiveColor from the RixBxdf-derived class.

Note   EmitLocal() provides the final color for the Bxdf plugin; thus, there is no numerical integration involved. The PDF value of a sample and Monte Carlo estimator are not relevant in the "emissive" Bxdf plugin.

The remaining member functions are only nominally implemented, usually with null functionality. These are as follows:

- SimpleEmissive::GetEvaluationDomain()

- SimpleEmissive::GetProperty()

- SimpleEmissive::GetAggregateLobeTraits()

- SimpleEmissive::GenerateSample()

- SimpleEmissive::EvaluateSample()

- SimpleEmissive::EvaluateSamplesAtIndex()

The m_emissiveColor array is set in the constructor. The renderer's global integrator instantiates the RixBxdf (closure) objects as part of the call to the factory's BeginScatter() member function interface.

Diffuse Reflection Model

Next, we talk about the perfect diffuse material. This is referred to as Lambertian[14] reflectance. See Figure 6-1. We assume energy conservation, that is

$$L_i = L_r + L_a + L_t$$

---

[14] Named after Johann Heinrich Lambert (1728–1777).

where L_i is irradiance (incident radiance), L_r is reflected radiance, L_a is absorbed radiance, and L_t is transmitted radiant energy. Note that for the simple diffuse model, L_t is not modeled and is therefore assumed to be zero.

Figure 6-1. *Diffuse Bxdf rendering using the RIB file in Listing 6-1 modified for the diffuse Bxdf plugin. The albedo color is [1.0, 1.0, 1.0]. The unlit portion is black, with the background not rendered*

The Lambertian BRDF is independent of ω_i or ω_r. It represents equal distribution of reflected radiance for all directions over the hemisphere of solid angle. The BRDF is

$$f\left(\omega_i,\omega_r\right)=\frac{\rho_r}{\pi}.$$

ρ_r is the total reflectance in the hemisphere (the albedo, a value between 0.0 and 1.0 for each of the red, green, or blue channels). It is scaled by π^{-1} to maintain energy conservation. This scaling factor is determined by evaluating

$$\rho_r = f\left(\omega_i,\omega_r\right)\int_{\Omega}cos\left(\theta_o\right)d\omega_o,$$

where f is constant and the right-hand side represents the reflected radiant radiance.[15]

---

[15] For more information on energy conservation and normalization for BRDF, see: Ian Mallett and Cem Yuksel. "Constant-time energy-normalization for the Phong specular BRDFs." *The Visual Computer* 36.10 (2020): 2029–2038. In particular, refer to the paper's Eq. 1.

> **Note**   The perfect diffuse reflector is easy to scale for energy conservation because the BRDF is constant. However, other BRDFs are not as easy to normalize. For example, Phong specular reflection is not trivially normalized so that it maintains both energy conservation and no loss of energy.

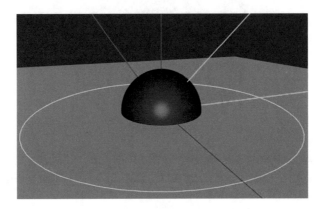

Figure 6-2.   Lambertian spherical plot. Red and green lines are the u and v surface directions. The blue line is the surface normal. Purple and cyan lines are the reflection and light directions, respectively. Radiant exitance is equally distributed over all directions. A spherical plot of this BRDF is often referred to as the "diffuse lobe"[16]

Diffuse Plugin Factory Class

Our diffuse factory class is similar to the emissive one but with an added `private` diffuse color member variable and diffuse lobe information, for example, `RixBXLobeSampled`- and `RixBXLobeTraits`-typed variables.

Bxdf lobe types are in the `Rix` API's *RixBxdfLobe.h*. RenderMan uses lobes for sampling the defined constituent parts of a BRDF. A single Bxdf plugin may contain multiple lobes. For instance, a "plastic" material exhibits both a diffuse and specular component. These are represented by two lobes (reflection regimes), otherwise known as a multilayered BRDF. RenderMan uses the `RixBXLobeTraits` `struct` to store information about the set of lobes a Bxdf supports and to properly sample the light field during scattering calculations.

---

[16] BRDF visualization is from the Disney BRDF Explorer (*https://github.com/wdas/brdf*).

Lobe variables are public and static. The renderer may call SimpleDiffuseBxdfPlugin::Synchronize() before calling SimpleDiffuseBxdfPlugin::BeginScatter(). See Listing 6-7.

SimpleDiffuseBxdfPlugin::GetIndexOfRefraction() returns a 1.0 for no refraction, although we do not implement or allow transmission.

Listing 6-7. SimpleDiffuseBxdfPlugin::Synchronize() from factory.h. The static lobe variables are set using RixBXLookupLobeByName()

```
void
SimpleDiffuseBxdfPlugin::Synchronize(RixContext& ctx, RixSCSyncMsg
syncMsg,RixParameterList const* parameterList)
{
    PIXAR_ARGUSED(ctx);
    PIXAR_ARGUSED(syncMsg);
    PIXAR_ARGUSED(parameterList);
    if (syncMsg == k_RixSCRenderBegin)
    {
        s_SimpleDiffuseLobe = RixBXLookupLobeByName(ctx, false,
            false, true, false,
            SimpleDiffuseBxdfPlugin::k_SimpleDiffuseLobeId,
            "Diffuse");
        s_SimpleDiffuseLobeTraits =
          RixBXLobeTraits(SimpleDiffuseBxdfPlugin::s_SimpleDiffuseLobe);
    }
}
```

Diffuse Plugin `RixBxdf` Class

While the Lambertian BRDF is constant, as seen in the previous section, the Bxdf plugin (not BRDF itself) is still responsible for calculating both an indirect sample from the light field using an appropriate PDF (with associated PDF value) and calculation of the dilution of the incident radiance (the cosine term).[17] See Listing 6-8, where information about the shade points is set in the `RixBxdf` object.

Listing 6-8. The `RixBxdf`-derived class `SimpleDiffuse`'s constructor from diffuse.cpp. We copy the shading context's array of shade point values from the shading context into member variables (boldface) of `SimpleDiffuse`. `m_lobesWanted` is set with bitwise AND'ing from the `static` `s_SimpleDiffuseLobeTraits RixBXLobeTraits` field of the factory

```
SimpleDiffuse::SimpleDiffuse(RixShadingContext const* sc,
     RixBxdfFactory* bx, RixBXLobeTraits const& lobesWanted,
     RtColorRGB const* diff):
          RixBxdf(sc, bx),
          m_lobesWanted(lobesWanted),
          m_diffuse_color(diff)
{
   RixBXLobeTraits lobes =
     SimpleDiffuseBxdfPlugin::s_SimpleDiffuseLobeTraits;
   m_lobesWanted &= lobes;
   sc->GetBuiltinVar(RixShadingContext::k_P, &m_P);
   sc->GetBuiltinVar(RixShadingContext::k_Nn, &m_Nn);
   sc->GetBuiltinVar(RixShadingContext::k_Tn, &m_Tn);
   sc->GetBuiltinVar(RixShadingContext::k_Vn, &m_Vn);
}
```

---

[17] Kajiya, James T. "The rendering equation." *Proceedings of the 13th annual conference on computer graphics and interactive techniques,* 1986. We first saw the rendering equation in Chapter 4.

The global integrator calls SimpleDiffuse::GenerateSample() between calls to SimpleDiffuseBxdfPlugin::BeginScatter() and SimpleDiffuseBxdfPlugin::EndScatter(). SimpleDiffuse::GenerateSample() must return an "indirect" normalized light direction, that is, the sample, for each shade point (thus, an array of RtVector3 objects). See Listing 6-9.

Listing 6-9. SimpleDiffuse's GenerateSample() is shown as follows. There are six "out" parameters (boldface). The member function returns whether the lobe is sampled or not in lobeSampled. Ln is the array of samples taken from either a uniform or cosine-distributed vector distribution over the hemisphere of solid angle. The sampling (and PDF value calculation) is performed in sampleLightField(). Note that this is a single-layer Bxdf, but GenerateSample() still checks for the "diffuse" lobe

```
void SimpleDiffuse::GenerateSample(
        RixBXTransportTrait transportTrait,
        RixBXLobeTraits const* lobesWanted,
        RixRNG * rng,

        // output:
        RixBXLobeSampled* lobeSampled,
        RtVector3 * Ln,
        RixBXLobeWeights& W,
        float* FPdf,
        float* RPdf,
        RtColorRGB * compTrans)
{
  int num_pts = shadingCtx->numPts;

  RixBXLobeTraits all = GetAllLobeTraits();
  RtFloat2* xi = (RtFloat2*)RixAlloca(sizeof(RtFloat2) * num_pts);
  rng->DrawSamples2D(xi);    // draw number of points 2D samples

  RtColorRGB* diff_wgt = NULL;

  for (int i = 0; i < num_pts; i++)
  {
    lobeSampled[i].SetValid(false);
```

```
    RixBXLobeTraits lobes = (all & lobesWanted[i]);
    bool SimpleDiffuse_lobe = (lobes &
    SimpleDiffuseBxdfPlugin::s_SimpleDiffuseLobeTraits).HasAny();

    if (!diff_wgt && SimpleDiffuse_lobe){
      diff_wgt =
      W.AddActiveLobe(SimpleDiffuseBxdfPlugin::s_SimpleDiffuseLobe);
    }

    if (SimpleDiffuse_lobe)
    {
      float NdV;
      NdV = m_Nn[i].Dot(m_Vn[i]);

      if (NdV > 0.0) {
        sampleLightField( NdV,
                          m_Nn[i],
                          m_Tn[i],
                          m_diffuse_color[i],
                          xi[i],

                          // output:
                          Ln[i],
                          diff_wgt[i],
                          FPdf[i],
                          RPdf[i] );

      lobeSampled[i].SetValid(true);
    }
    else {
      lobeSampled[i].SetValid(false);
    }
  }
}
}
```

In addition to `SimpleDiffuse::GenerateSample()`, there are two other member functions in `SimpleDiffuse` that are defined for evaluation after the light sample has been determined. These are as follows:

- `SimpleDiffuse::EvaluateSample()`

- `SimpleDiffuse::EvaluateSamplesAtIndex()`[18]

Not unless the integrator must generate many light samples for a single shade point is `SimpleDiffuse::EvaluateSamplesAtIndex()` called. See Listing 6-10 for `SimpleDiffuse::EvaluateSample()`. This member function checks the lobe's request, then if the light vector is above the plane of the differential area.

Note `GenerateSample()` and `EvaluateSample()` implementations are usually very similar. They both must query the requested lobe and loop through each shade point. However, `GenerateSample()` is called by the global integrator before `EvaluateSample()` for a given shading context. Indirect light samples need to be generated first to evaluate their light contributions in `EvaluateSample()`.

Listing 6-10. `SimpleDiffuse::EvaluateSample()`. This is a required member function. Our Bxdf calculation is "squirreled" away in `evaluateBRDF()`. We ignore back-facing surfaces, those whose normal is greater than 90 degrees from the light ray direction, or $N \cdot L > 90$ degrees

```
void SimpleDiffuse::EvaluateSample(
     RixBXTransportTrait transportTrait,
     RixBXLobeTraits const* lobesWanted,
     RixRNG * rng,
     RixBXLobeTraits * lobesEvaluated,   // a result
     RtVector3 const* Ln,
```

---

[18] See the book's code repository for `SimpleDiffuse::EvaluateSamplesAtIndex()`.

```
        // output:
        RixBXLobeWeights & W,
        float* FPdf,
        float* RPdf)
{
  PIXAR_ARGUSED(transportTrait);
  PIXAR_ARGUSED(rng);

  int num_pts = shadingCtx->numPts;
  RixBXLobeTraits all = GetAllLobeTraits();

  RtColorRGB* diff_wgt = NULL;

  for (int i = 0; i < num_pts; i++)
  {
    lobesEvaluated[i].SetNone();
    RixBXLobeTraits lobes = (all & lobesWanted[i]);
    bool diff_lobe = (lobes &
      SimpleDiffuseBxdfPlugin::s_SimpleDiffuseLobeTraits).HasAny();

    if (!diff_wgt && diff_lobe) {
      diff_wgt =
      W.AddActiveLobe(SimpleDiffuseBxdfPlugin::s_SimpleDiffuseLobe);
    }

    if ( diff_lobe )
    {
      float NdV;

      NdV = m_Nn[i].Dot(m_Vn[i]);

      if (NdV > 0.0) {
        float NdL = m_Nn[i].Dot(Ln[i]);

        if (NdL > 0.f) {
          evaluateBRDF( NdV,
                        NdL,
                        m_diffuse_color[i],
                        m_Nn[i],
```

```
                    Ln[i],
                    m_Vn[i],

                    // output:
                    diff_wgt[i],
                    FPdf[i],
                    RPdf[i] );

          lobesEvaluated[i] |=
            SimpleDiffuseBxdfPlugin::s_SimpleDiffuseLobeTraits;

          lobesEvaluated[i].SetValid(true);
        } else {
          lobesEvaluated[i].SetValid(false);
        }
      }
    }
  }
}
```

PDF Selection and Sampling

For all of our sample PDF descriptions, we use a cosine distribution of light samples about the unit normal. The Rix provides an API function that generates a vector using this distribution via RixCosDirectionalDistribution().

This *RixShadingUtils.h* Rix API function requires two random numbers, from the xi parameter,[19] plus the tangent and normal (for a given shade point) as provided by the shading context to the constructor back. We determine the tangent space vector first, however, using RixComputeShadingBasis(). See Listing 6-11.

The details of the RixCosDirectionalDistribution() Rix API function can be found in *RixShadingUtils.h* of the Rix API headers.

---

[19] See Chapter 8 for an explanation of PDF and sampling computations.

Listing 6-11. sampleLightField(). Calls to RixCosDirectionalDistribution() are in boldface, as well as the estimator value for the light sample. This is the diffuse color multiplied by the PDF based on the cosine distribution

```
PRMAN_INLINE
void SimpleDiffuse::sampleLightField(float NdV,
                                     const RtNormal3& Nn,
                                     const RtVector3& Tn,
                                     const RtColorRGB& diff,
                                     const RtFloat2& xi,

                                     // output:
                                     RtVector3& Ln,
                                     RtColorRGB& W,
                                     float& FPdf,
                                     float& RPdf)
{
    RtVector3 TX, TY;
    RixComputeShadingBasis(Nn, Tn, TX, TY);

    float NdL;
    RixCosDirectionalDistribution(xi, Nn, TX, TY, Ln, NdL);

    // cosine distribution pdfs
    FPdf = NdL * F_INVPI;
    RPdf = NdV * F_INVPI;

    W = diff * FPdf;
}
```

Note   W = diff * FPdf is not the weight of the value of the integrand. This is
the weight in the Monte Carlo estimator for the sample of the integrand using the
generated light field sample. We calculate the integrand sample itself for the BRDF
geometry in evaluateSample() or evaluateSamplesAtIndex(). Realize
also that in the evaluate*() routines, the plugin does not know the incoming
radiance, only the generated light field sample direction (normalized) from another
RixBxdf object. We will see this again when we discuss the PxrValidateBxdf
global integrator in Chapter 7.

In Listing 6-12, we see the implementation for SimpleDiffuse::evaluateBRDF(). We
must multiply the diffuse differential radiance output with the cosine term. Recall that
the BRDF is the ratio of outgoing radiance to incident irradiance directions.

Listing 6-12. evaluateBRDF(). We calculate the outgoing radiance in W from
the incident irradiance over the input solid angle. The output parameters are
shown in boldface. In Chapter 7, we introduce an error in calculating the RPdf
value shown here using a uniform distribution PDF value instead of the cosine
distribution, where the sample is assigned a lower PDF value.[20]

```
PRMAN_INLINE
void SimpleDiffuse::evaluateBRDF(float NdV,
                                 float NdL,
                                 const RtColorRGB& diff,
                                 const RtVector3 Nn,
                                 const RtVector3 Ln,
                                 const RtVector3 Vn,

                                 // output:
                                 RtColorRGB& W,
                                 float& FPdf,
                                 RtFloat& RPdf)
```

---

[20] This helps to illustrate the use of the global integrator PxrValidateBxdf in finding errors in the
Bxdf calculations.

```
{
    // cosine distribution pdfs
    FPdf = NdL * F_INVPI;
    RPdf = NdV * F_INVPI;

    // diffuse reflection constant
    // (see renderning eq.) with light dilution
    W = diff * F_INVPI * NdL;
}
```

Note   RixBxdf is a bit of a misnomer. We need to include the $N \cdot L$ term for light dilution.

Specular Reflection Model

The specular model (SimpleSpecularBxdfFactory and SimpleSpecular classes) is implemented similarly to the diffuse one. Lobe information is likewise contained as static variables in the factory and written to the RixBxdf object by the factory's Synchronize() member function. The plugin's source code is included in the following four files:

- *factory.h*
- *factory.cpp*
- *specular.h*
- *specular.cpp*

We use Phong's specular component BRDF calculation,[21] and it is performed in the evaluateSamples() member function of SimpleSpecular. See the rendering in Figure 6-3. The specular lobe visualization is shown in Figure 6-4. The random light sample vector is chosen from RixCosDirectionalDistribution() in the *specular.cpp* using the same FPdf and RPdf values as in our diffuse Bxdf plugin.

---

[21] Phong, Bui Tuong. "Illumination for computer generated pictures." *Communications of the ACM* 18.6 (1975): 311–317.

Figure 6-3. *Specular Bxdf rendering. The specular color is [0.0, 0.8, 0.6], with the gloss exponent set at 200. The unlit portion is black, with the background not rendered*

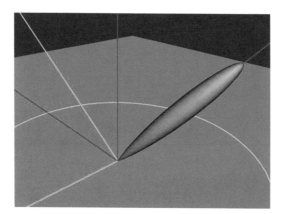

Figure 6-4. *Specular BRDF in spherical plot. The red and green lines are the u and v surface directions; the blue line is the surface normal. Purple and cyan lines are the reflection and light directions, respectively. Radiant exitance is not equally distributed. It is centered on the reflection vector. A spherical plot of this BRDF is often referred to as the "specular lobe"*[22]

---

[22] BRDF visualization is performed via the Disney BRDF Explorer. See *https://github.com/wdas/brdf*

Note   Our Bxdf implementation does not scale (multiply) the modified Phong BRDF by $\frac{n+2}{2\pi}$ to maintain energy conservation.[23] In order to be physically accurate, this BRDF should not reflect more light than is incident on the differential surface.

Plastic (Phong) Material

This chapter's code examples include a third plugin. It is for a "plastic" material using a composite of both diffuse and specular lobes (multilayered). The plugin uses a linear combination of the separate BRDFs. RIB parameters for the mixing are also implemented. Figure 6-5 shows the combined lobes.

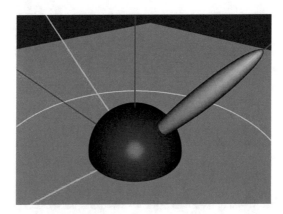

Figure 6-5. *Combined (multilayer) "plastic" BRDF in spherical plot. The red and green lines are the u and v surface directions; the blue line is the surface normal. Purple and cyan lines are the reflection and light directions, respectively*

---

[23] For more information on energy conservation and normalization for the Phong BRDF, see: Ian Mallett and Cem Yuksel. "Constant-time energy-normalization for the Phong specular BRDFs." *The Visual Computer* 36.10 (2020): 2029–2038. In particular, see the paper's Eqs. 4–6.

For the plugin to conserve energy, the sum of the diffuse and specular color component weights for each individual channel must not exceed 1.0. That is, ρ_d (diffuse color weights) and ρ_s (specular color weights) must not exceed 1.0. That is

$$\rho_d + \rho_s \leq [\, 1.0, 1.0, 1, 0 \,].$$

Summary

In this chapter, we have covered basic reflection types and how these are implemented as Bxdf plugins. We also showed how distribution sampling is needed in modern Bxdf plugins. In Chapter 8, we will discuss sampling and PDF determination in greater depth.

CHAPTER 7

Developing and Debugging Bxdf

This chapter explains how Bxdf plugins may be developed. We cover the use of a visual debugger front end, along with some of the facilities of RenderMan (e.g., PxrValidateBxdf).[1] We also discuss the notion of dynamically loaded (shared objects) libraries.

Thus, in this chapter, we go into the practicalities of setting up a development environment. One aspect of using C++, rather than RSL, is that we can take full advantage of system-level development. These allow for halting the process at various breakpoints and inspecting the plugin's state (variable values, etc.). Because RixBxdf objects run in multiple threads during rendering, we show how to step through a single thread so that debugging may be performed in a similar fashion to serial execution development.

Development Environments

While development can take place on Linux,[2] macOS, and Windows, many of these platforms offer platform-specific IDEs. These prominently include Xcode (Apple) and Visual Studio (Microsoft Windows). IDEs usually contain a visual front end to a debugger, allowing interactive use of breakpoints with call-stack information.

In this book, we choose VS Code, a cross-platform IDE. VS Code is freely available on all major OS platforms and can be used simply by opening a directory containing your plugin code. Thus, it is more lightweight and reminiscent of more traditional text editors

---

[1] We spent time in Chapter 2 discussing C++ and the make utility.
[2] Usually CentOS but also Ubuntu per the installation from Chapter 1.

© Brad E. Hollister 2023
B. E. Hollister, *Essential Guide to RenderMan® Shading Plugin Development*,
https://doi.org/10.1007/978-1-4842-9392-8_7

such as Vim or Emacs.[3] For instance, when you install Mingw-w64 (for use of the make utility on Windows), you can use the following modified Makefile from Chapter 2. See Listing 7-1.

Listing 7-1. Recall our discussion about Makefiles from Chapter 2. We see a slightly modified version for use with the MSVC compiler cl.[4] The make utility for Windows installs via MSYS2 and a single plugin is implemented in two source files (Chapter 6). We need to use the link command to generate dlls on the Windows platform, and we define the WIN32 macro to include the proper memory allocation standard runtime system libraries. These changes are in boldface. Finally, we use del to remove a prior build's obj files.

```
CC = cl
CFLAGS = -Z7 -nologo -MD -EHsc -D"WIN32=1"
INCLUDES = -I"$(RMANTREE)\include"
LIBS = "$(RMANTREE)\lib\libpxrcore.lib"
LD = link -DEBUG -nologo -DLL

SOURCES = \
    diffuse.cpp \
    factory.cpp

PLUGIN = diffuse.dll

OBJECTS = $(SOURCES:.cpp=.obj)
.SUFFIXES: .cpp .obj .dll

all: $(OBJECTS)
    $(LD) -out:"$(PLUGIN)" $^ $(LIBS)
```

---

[3] In Chapter 2, Makefiles were introduced because the official Pixar example plugin source code comes with Makefiles. However, Makefiles are not native to Windows. You may install the MSYS2 tools and libraries, however. See *https://msys2.org* and *https://code.visualstudio.com/docs/cpp/config-mingw*.

[4] Direct use of a platform compiler is provided on the Pixar website under their official documentation. We include some additional information here about Windows, as Windows has the most options and requires changes to Pixar's official demo plugin Makefiles.

```
.cpp.obj: $(SOURCES)
    $(CC) $(INCLUDES) $(CFLAGS) -c $^

.PHONY: clean

clean:
    del *.obj *.ilk
```

Note   Be sure to provide proper flags for compiling debug information into your plugin object files (via -Z7)[5] and to include the -DEBUG option to the linker.

Listing 7-2. From the Rix API header RixShadingUtils.h. The WIN32 macro switch is shown for compiling on Windows.[6]

```
#if defined(WIN32)
#include <malloc.h>
#include <intrin.h>
#else
#include <alloca.h>
#endif
```

Visual Debugging with Multiple Threads

As shown in Listing 7-1, you should compile your plugins by including debug information in the object files (at least during development). This is done with the switches (flags) passed to the compiler and linker, respectively.

With RSL, it was impossible to use a debugger to stop execution and inspect a call stack. However, with C++, we can use the full set of system-level debugging tools. The exact debugger will depend on your platform (e.g., gdb).

---

[5] See *https://learn.microsoft.com/en-us/cpp/build/reference/z7-zi-zi-debug-information-format?source=recommendations&view=msvc-170* for more details on the flags that can be passed to cl and link on Windows, which can affect the size of object files, and if there are program database files (pdb).

[6] You can configure VS Code to work with either the gcc from Ubuntu WSL or MSYS2, as mentioned in a prior footnote. For more info on WSL and VS Code, see *https://code.visualstudio.com/docs/cpp/config-wsl*

Figure 7-1. *Debugging with breakpoints in multiple threads for Bxdf development using VS Code.[7] This was configured using a launch.json script (included in the source code for the chapter). Code shown is from a file called PxrDiffuse2.cpp, altered from a sample file from Pixar*

Note   When debugging multi-threaded code, in order to maintain serial execution stepping, the initial breakpoint must be deactivated so that subsequent threads do not break while you are executing in the thread of interest. Once a breakpoint is hit for your thread, deactivate it so that you can continue executing serially in that thread only.

---

[7] A launch.json file resides in the .vscode, at the top of your "workspace" directory. Depending on your toolset (on Windows), you may need to use either "cppvsdebug" (for MSVC tools) or "cppdebug" (for MSYS2 GNU compiler and debugger). These are possible values for the "type" field within the launch.json file.

The renderman.ini File

Once you have built your plugin, you need to set a path to it in *renderman.ini*.[8] prman will load it, to be used in a rendering session. There are a number of *renderman.ini* settings. But for starters, the most significant is /standardrixpluginpath. The default value is ${RMANTREE}/lib/plugins. You may add (concatenate) additional paths by separating each path by a colon. An example is shown in Listing 7-3.

Listing 7-3. Relevant settings (elided renderman.ini) for providing a path to your Bxdf plugins. The paths for Rix plugins are in boldface—with an additional path separated by a colon.

```
...
# settings commonly customized for a site
/standardshaderpath  ${RMANTREE}/lib/shaders:${RMSTREE}/lib/shaders
/standardrixpluginpath      ${RMANTREE}/lib/plugins:C:/Users/cscco/
devstuff/pixar/Debug
/standardrifpath ${RMANTREE}/lib/plugins
/prman/statistics/xmlfilename
/prman/textureformat  tiff
...
```

Note   prman will search the paths in the order they are listed. If you have a plugin with the same name in more than one path, the first path's copy will be used. Also, the name of the Bxdf in the RIB is the name of the plugin's .so or .dll file.

VS Code Extensions for RIB and RSL

It is often helpful to work first with RSL, to simplify the initial development of a Bxdf. Once a local lighting version is created using RSL, you then translate it to a C++ plugin for use with the NCR. This can be facilitated using the extension "RSL-Language" for VS Code. Another is a "RIB For Renderman," which colorizes your RIB files. Both are shown in Figure 7-2.

---

[8] This is in your NCR server's installation directory, that is, *${RMANTREE}/etc*.

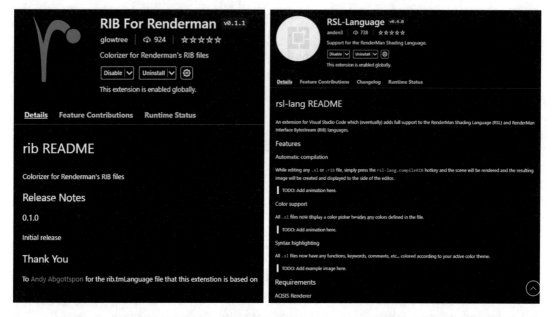

Figure 7-2. *The VS Code extension called "RIB For Renderman" by glowtree (left). The "RSL-Language" VS Code extension by anden3 (right) assumes the use of Aqsis,[9] an open source RenderMan-compliant renderer using RSL*

Using PxrValidateBxdf

A primary purpose of PxrValidateBxdf (global integrator) is to ensure that all lobe weights in a Bxdf plugin add to 1.0. Recall that a multilayer Bxdf may have up to eight separate lobes, each of type "diffuse," "specular," or "user-defined." The total for each color channel, over all lobes (Bxdf layers), should not exceed 1.0.

Note   Simple Bxdf, like the ones already described in Chapter 6, all have only one or two total lobes. PxrValidateBxdf is less helpful in those cases. A single lobe Bxdf will use a single weight. If you do not set a lobe as sampled in GenerateSample(), with its RixBXLobeSampled parameter, PxrValidateBxdf will skip past those shade points and output 0.0 for its color channel results.[10]

---

[9] For more information on Aqsis, see *https://github.com/aqsis/aqsis*, *www.aqsis.org/*, and *https://en.wikipedia.org/wiki/Aqsis*

[10] Some of the Pixar examples (such as, PxrDiffuse) do not set their single lobe as sampled, therefore these will produce null results when testing with PxrValidateBxdf.

PxrValidateBxdf, in ValidateBxdfWorker::Integrate(), sums the output values of GenerateSample() for each shade point. It divides out the PDF importance sample weight, averages lobe weights, takes the luminance (the sum of the red, green, and blue divided by the number of color channels), and renders this in the red channel.

All visible surface shade points, irrespective of light samples, should have the same luminance (red channel value). If not, the Bxdf has output inconsistent values for the lobe weights for the generated samples. See Figure 7-3.

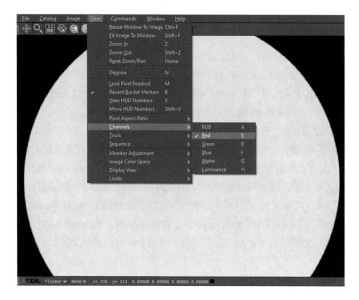

Figure 7-3. *Selecting the "red" channel with* it, *after a render of our basic RIB using* PxrValidateBxdf. *What is shown is the luminance (average of all color channels' weights) for a single diffuse lobe. In the lower window tray, we see numerical values for each color channel, including alpha*

Additionally, PxrValidateBxdf outputs a blue and green channel luminance. The green channel output of PxrValidateBxdf provides the weight computed by your Bxdf in the EvaluateSample() routine for the samples from GenerateSample().

GenerateSample()'s forward PDF is EvaluateSamples()'s reverse PDF for a given shade point (i.e., render context). Because PxrValidateBxdf factors out the PDF value in its luminance averaging for the blue channel, the results should be the same, unless different PDFs were assigned in the separate member functions. Also, the luminance should be less than or equal to 1.0 and likely uniformly less than the red channel.

The blue channel contains the results of the global integrator using a cosine distribution and calling `EvaluateSample()` on the Bxdf. See Figure 7-4 for an example error detected by `PxrValidateBxdf`.

Figure 7-4. *`PxrValidateBxdf` rendering for the red channel (left), green channel (middle), and blue channel (right) for the simple diffuse Bxdf plugin example in Chapter 6. `PxrValidateBxdf` allows for setting the number of samples. The number of samples in the example is four (default value). An error in our simple diffuse plugin was introduced, where a uniform reverse PDF was used in `EvaluateSample()`. It should be a cosine distribution, as used in `GenerateSample()`. Therefore, a lower-than-expected blue channel luminance uncovers this issue, as the red and blue channels should be identical. The blue channel uses weights (reverse PDFs) from a cosine distribution created from the global integrator `PxrValidateBxdf` itself. Therefore, the red and blue channels match, as they were both using samples from a cosine distribution*

Using `PxrDebugShadingContext`

`PxrDebugShadingContext` is another useful global integrator for developing. Suppose you are not seeing a surface that only reflects on one side, that is, `k_RixBXOutsideReflect` is returned from your factory's `GetEvaluationDomain()`.

One way to help debug this would be to use `PxrDebugShadingContext` to render the `InsideOutside` value from the shading context. See Figure 7-5. You can also render many other fields in the shading context (such as `Nn` and `Vn`) for each of the shade points.

Figure 7-5. *The PxrDebugShadingContext's InsideOutside maps green to outside values—the cosine of the angle between the viewing direction and the surface normal—when it is positive*

Summary

This chapter provides guidance on using VS Code for developing Bxdf plugins.[11] We discussed another sample Makefile, setting up *renderman.ini*, so that prman knows where to locate your compiled plugin. We also talked about how to navigate a visual debugger to break on a single thread.

In this chapter, we showed how PxrValidateBxdf and PxrDebugShadingContext can be used for providing viewable output.[12]

---

[11] We did not discuss the Args XML file and tools, such as the use of Blender's RenderMan add-on.

[12] Additionally, we did not include the global integrator PxrVisualize in our consideration. While this global integrator plugin may be of use, its output is not directly related to a Bxdf.

CHAPTER 8

PDF Normalization, Sampling, and Anisotropic Bxdf

This chapter concludes the book with some representative anisotropic Bxdf plugins.

First, though, we start by describing step by step how to calculate the PDF for the uniform and cosine distributions about a hemisphere and how to draw random vectors from those distributions. This was previously only discussed at a high level to allow for focusing on the RenderMan execution environment. However, a PDF value is required whenever you are "generating" samples or "evaluating" them in the Monte Carlo RenderMan framework for Bxdf.

Next, we focus on anisotropic Bxdf, specifically Ward (single specular lobe) and Marschner's finished wood material. The latter is interesting, in that it is an example of a BSSDF (Bidirectional Surface Scattering Function) but treated as an intrinsic material property.[1] It is also multilayered, exhibiting two specular lobes and a diffuse one.[2] Each of the Bxdf plugins in this chapter has accompanying RSL code[3] (see the book's repository) for those making the transition from RSL to Bxdf plugins, or using RSL in parallel with Bxdf development.

---

[1] A possible extension is to "split up" our finished wood Bxdf using transmission. However, as this book is an introduction to writing Bxdf, we forgo such a treatment.

[2] Note that its diffuse and surface specular lobes are essentially the same as those depicted separately in Chapter 6. For visualizations, see the corresponding figures from that chapter. The BSSDF's subsurface (fiber) specular lobe is depicted diagrammatically in Marschner, Stephen R., et al. "Measuring and modeling the appearance of finished wood." *ACM SIGGRAPH 2005 Papers*, 2005, 727–734.

[3] As noted already, the RSL code can be used with a RenderMan-compliant open source renderer such as Aqsis (*https://github.com/aqsis/aqsis*). In many cases, this is a natural starting place for Bxdf development, as the framework and execution model is simpler to test initial ideas.

B. E. Hollister, *Essential Guide to RenderMan® Shading Plugin Development*, https://doi.org/10.1007/978-1-4842-9392-8_8

PDFs and Sampling

We have already discussed the Monte Carlo estimator in the context of the rendering equation. However, we have yet to show explicitly how to calculate (normalize) a PDF from an arbitrary analytic function whose profile is similar (some common factor usually) with the rendering equation's integrand.[4]

Before proceeding, you may want to review topics from Chapters 3, 4, and 6 on related topics for a review. Let us start with a uniform distribution about the hemisphere.

Note   Importance sampling from a uniform distribution is almost never performed in a path tracer, as the use of a cosine distribution converges more quickly (less variance). The reason is that the rendering equation always contains a cosine term evaluated for the angle between the surface normal and the light vector. However, we use the uniform distribution over the hemisphere to illustrate the normalization process. For all of the following steps, you would simply substitute for *k* a function of whose profile you want to consider as a PDF in your Monte Carlo estimators. Realize that in the general case, *k* is not constant, and the integration would need to be performed accordingly.

PDF Normalization

A uniform PDF will have a single (constant) value for every light vector direction in our domain. This direction, ω, has two components. The first is θ, which is in the interval $\left[0, \dfrac{\pi}{2}\right]$, and represents the angle between the surface normal and ω.

The second component, ϕ, is in the range $[0, 2\pi]$. This is the angle ω makes with surface direction **u** (orthogonal to the surface normal and usually thought of as the canonical x-direction when transforming to spherical coordinates from a Cartesian basis). See Figure 8-1.

---

[4] Recall that we do not know the "light field," or incoming radiance, which is part of the integrand, until we trace rays through the scene. Thus, the cosine term, and potentially the BRDF itself, may be used and then normalized for the interval of the upper hemisphere.

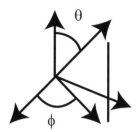

Figure 8-1. *Decomposition of the components (θ, φ) of ω. The surface normal is in the canonical Cartesian direction of z (or "up") in the diagram*

We only know (at the moment) that the PDF will be constant. We start with an arbitrary PDF function, *k*, and integrate it over the measure, or domain *Ω* (i.e., the upper hemisphere), like so:

$$\int_{\Omega} k \, d\omega.$$

After expressing the preceding integral in its component form and moving the constant term outside the integral, we get

$$k \int_{0}^{2\pi} \int_{0}^{\frac{\pi}{2}} sin \, \theta \, d\theta d\phi.$$

Recall that *dω* is the differential solid angle of a hemisphere with a unit radius. Therefore, *dω* represents the differential surface area on the unit-hemisphere. The computation of *dω* is shown in Figure 8-2.

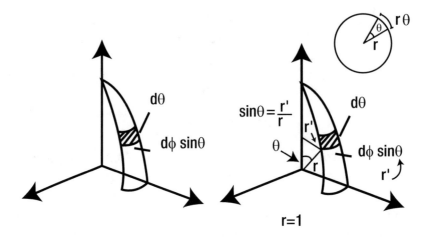

Figure 8-2. *The area dω is the product of its linear "width" and "height." The diagram on the right is embellished. For differential quantities, curvature is considered linear (known as "in-the-small"). Thus, dω = dθdφsin θ. Note that r = 1, simplifying our equations, as the arc length represented by dθ (the "height") is rdθ. As differential dω gets closer to the "north" pole of the hemisphere, the "width" gets smaller as factor sin θ, which is the radius of the cross-sectional circle perpendicular to the normal ("z") direction. Recall that the arc length of a circle is the product of the radius and angle in radians subtended by the arc at the center of a circle*

Now that we have our integral, we just need to invoke the fundamental theorem of calculus, which allows us to evaluate it as a closed-form (analytic) solution. We have

$$k \int_0^{2\pi} d\phi \int_0^{\frac{\pi}{2}} \sin\theta \ d\theta = -2\pi k \left(\cos\frac{\pi}{2} - \cos 0 \right),$$

or $2\pi k$.

In order to find the normalization constant to determine our uniform PDF over the hemisphere, we simply set the integral to 1, which is the sum of all probability densities over our measure (the upper hemisphere's solid angle). That is, $2\pi k = 1$, where $k = \dfrac{1}{2\pi}$. Therefore, the PDF value (probability density) for any randomly chosen light vector sample chosen from a uniform PDF is $\dfrac{1}{2\pi}$.

Cosine Distribution

PDF normalization is the same process for other functions. As a second example, consider the cosine distribution.[5]

Note   For all of the Bxdf plugins written in this book, the cosine-distributed PDF and importance sampling are used.

We start with the following:

$$\int_\Omega cos\ \theta\ d\omega.$$

After our coordinate transform to spherical coordinates, we have

$$\int_0^{2\pi} d\phi \int_0^{\frac{\pi}{2}} cos\ \theta\ sin\ \theta\ d\theta = 2\pi \int_0^{\frac{\pi}{2}} cos\ \theta\ sin\ \theta\ d\theta.$$

This is similar to the uniform distribution, but the integrand is not constant anymore. It varies with (i.e., "a function of") θ. Using the "double-angle" formula $sin(2\theta) = 2\ sin\ \theta\ cos\ \theta$, we have

$$2\pi \int_0^{\frac{\pi}{2}} cos\ \theta\ sin\ \theta\ d\theta = 2\left(\frac{1}{2}\right)\pi \int_0^{\frac{\pi}{2}} sin(2\theta)\ d\theta.$$

Substituting for 2θ (i. e. , $\theta' = 2\theta$), we get

$$\pi \int_0^{\frac{\pi}{2}} sin(2\theta)\ d\theta =$$

$$\pi \int_0^{\pi} sin(\theta')\ d\left(\frac{\theta'}{2}\right) = \frac{1}{2}\pi \int_0^{\pi} sin(\theta')\ d\theta',$$

---

[5] Try finding other PDFs that contain your BRDF, as an exercise.

and finally,

$$\frac{1}{2}\pi\int_{0}^{\pi}sin(\theta')\,d\theta' = -\frac{1}{2}\pi(cos\,\pi - cos\,0) = \pi.$$

Therefore, to normalize the original integral of $cos\,\theta$, we only need to divide it by π in order to meet the requirement that the sum of all probability densities over the continuous hemisphere of solid angle is 1.

As an exercise,[6] you might verify that our $PDF(\theta,\phi) = \dfrac{cos\,\theta}{\pi}$ by integrating over the hemisphere of solid angle. That is, show that

$$\int_{\Omega}\frac{cos\,\theta}{\pi}\,d\omega = 1.$$

Note   You will see that the `FPdf` ("forward" PDF)[7] and `RPdf` ("reverse" PDF) in the source code for this book use the PDF $\dfrac{cos\,\theta}{\pi}$, where the $cos\,\theta$ value is either the dot product between the normalized normal and the light vector, or normalized sample (view) vector divided by the *RixShadingUtils.h*'s constant macro `F_INVPI` (for inverse floating-point π value).

Sampling via the PDF

In this section, we demonstrate the use of the CDF, that is, the "cumulative (probability) density function,"[8] for sampling via a PDF. The CDF is just the integral of the PDF, which we have already indirectly illustrated in the previous section, when normalizing profile curves for use as PDF.

---

[6] This is trivial, as we already performed the integral on $cos\,\theta$ to find π.

[7] Concerns the direction of the samples when either generating or evaluating samples in the `RixBxdf` member functions `GenerateSample()` and `EvaluateSample()`, or the `EvaluateSamplesAtIndex()`.

[8] Oftentimes referred to as the cumulative distribution function.

Understanding this method is not strictly necessary if you are only using a cosine distribution for your Monte Carlo estimators. The utility function from *RixShadingUtils.h*, namely, `RixCosDirectionalDistribution()`, returns a sample vector for you using the cosine distribution PDF (as mentioned in Chapters 4 and 6).

But if you choose to do your own importance sampling with a different PDF (one that is closer to your rendering equation's integrand), then knowing how this method works is essential. See Listing 8-1 for an example from the Bxdf plugins in this chapter.

Listing 8-1. Illustration of an indirect light field sample using `RixCosDirectionalDistribution()`. This `Rix` API utility returns the sample `Ln` in terms of the local Cartesian coordinate system. Later in this chapter, we will discuss how to generate the light sample's direction in local spherical coordinates. A simple coordinate transform from spherical to Cartesian is still required, if done manually (i.e., not using a utility function that handles this for you)

```
PRMAN_INLINE
void Ward::sampleLightFieldAllLobes(float NdV,
        const RtNormal3& Nn,
        const RtVector3& Tn,
        const RtColorRGB& reflected,
        const RtFloat2& xi,

        // output:
        RtVector3& Ln,
        RtColorRGB& W,
        float& FPdf,
        float& RPdf)
{
    RtVector3 TX, TY;
    RixComputeShadingBasis(Nn, Tn, TX, TY);

    float NdL;
    RixCosDirectionalDistribution(xi, Nn, TX, TY, Ln, NdL);
```

```
// cosine distribution pdf values
FPdf = NdL * F_INVPI;
RPdf = NdV * F_INVPI;

W = reflected * FPdf;
}
```

The procedure is listed as follows.[9] See Figure 8-3 for a visual representation.

1. Integrate to find $CDF(\theta, \phi)$.

2. Generate a random number from the canonical (continuous) uniform distribution.[10]

   a. This is just a number from 0 to 1, where each value in that range has equal probability density of being selected. In general, we denote this as $U_{[0, 1]}$.

3. Set the marginal CDF of ϕ, that is, $CDF(\theta, \phi_{max})$, to the value $U_{[0, 1], 1}$ (found in step 2) and solve for θ, which we call θ_{sample}.

4. Now, using the bivariate CDF, use its cross section at θ_{sample} over ϕ, that is, find $CDF(\theta_{sample}, \phi)$.

   a. Note, however, that this cross section integrated over ϕ will not necessarily reach 1, that is, $CDF(\theta_{sample}, \phi_{max}) \leq 1$, as it is only a cross section of the full bivariate CDF. Therefore, you need to scale by the cross-sectional integral, that is, find $U_{[0, 1], 2}CDF(\theta_{sample}, \phi_{max})$, where $U_{[0, 1], 2}$ denotes a second uniform random variable value from 0 to 1 inclusive.

5. Now, solve for ϕ from $CDF(\theta_{sample}, \phi) = U_{[0, 1], 2}CDF(\theta_{sample}, \phi_{max})$, which we call ϕ_{sample}.

---

[9] The bivariate inverse CDF for sampling is described in other texts as well. See:

Matt Pharr, Wenzel Jakob, and Greg Humphreys. *Physically based rendering: From theory to implementation*. Morgan Kaufmann, 2016.

Philip Dutre, Kavita Bala, and Philippe Bekaert. *Advanced global illumination*. AK Peters/CRC Press, 2018.

Peter Shirley and R. Keith Morley. *Realistic ray tracing*. AK Peters, Ltd., 2008.

[10] See *https://en.wikipedia.org//wiki/Continuous_uniform_distribution*

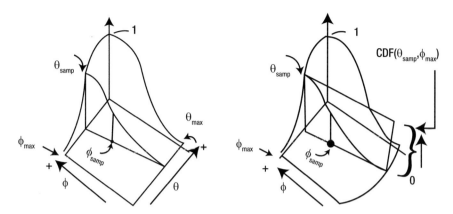

Figure 8-3. *Illustration of the bivariate CDF and cross section at θ_{sample}. On the left, we see basic labeling, and on the right, CDF(θ_{sample}, ϕ_{max}) is shown. We must scale our canonical $U_{[0,1],2}$ by CDF(θ_{sample}, ϕ_{max}), that is, the value at the margin of the graph labeled with θ_{sample}. In general, CDF(θ_{sample}, ϕ_{max}) is less than 1, unless our CDF($U_{[0,1],1}$, ϕ_{max}) is 1 because of the random variable $U_{[0,1],1}$ = 1. The arrows show increasing values of θ and ϕ, where θ_{max} and ϕ_{max} are at the margins*

An example using $PDF(\theta,\phi) = \dfrac{\cos\theta}{\pi}$ is shown in the following. We have already

calculated the integral $\int_{\Omega}\cos\theta\,d\omega$, so this is just repeated for the integrand $\dfrac{\cos\theta}{\pi}$. In

this example, however, we do not perform a "change of variables" over the measure as we did in the previous normalization. We want to preserve the domain for our random components. Thus, we integrate using the chain rule (or more specifically use the results of the chain rule to realize the proper antiderivative of the integrand).

In calculating our CDF, recall our integrand $cos\,\theta\,sin\,\theta$ for the PDF after transforming into spherical coordinates,[11] that is

$$CDF(\theta,\phi) = \int \frac{cos\,\theta'}{\pi}\,d\omega' =$$

$$\frac{1}{\pi}\int_0^\phi d\phi'\int_0^\theta cos\,\theta'\,sin\,\theta'\,d\theta'.$$

---

[11] Here, we substitute θ' and ϕ' for θ and ϕ so that we can use for the limits of integration the unprimed original notation. This is not strict substitution of variables but only preserves the parameter notation for the CDF.

Before proceeding, note that for $cos^2\theta$, we have

$$f(\theta) = cos^2\theta + constant,$$

and

$$\frac{df(\theta)}{d\theta} = -2cos\,\theta\,sin\,\theta.$$

To find the CDF, we use the preceding antiderivative, continuing with

$$\frac{1}{\pi}\int_0^\phi d\phi'\int_0^\theta cos\,\theta'\,sin\,\theta'\,d\theta' =$$

$$\frac{1}{\pi}\int_0^\phi d\phi'\int_0^\theta \left(-\frac{1}{2}\right)(-2)cos\,\theta'\,sin\,\theta'\,d\theta'$$

$$= -\frac{1}{2}\frac{\phi-0}{\pi}\int_0^\theta (-2)cos\,\theta'\,sin\,\theta'\,d\theta'$$

$$= -\frac{1}{2}\frac{\phi}{\pi}\left(cos^2\theta - cos^2 0\right)$$

$$= \frac{\phi}{2\pi}\left(1 - cos^2\theta\right).$$

Thus, our $CDF(\theta,\phi) = \dfrac{\phi}{2\pi}\left(1 - cos^2\theta\right)$. Applying the process and generating our first canonical random number, $U_{[0,1],1}$, we first solve for θ from $CDF(\theta,\phi_{max})$. That is, we need to find θ_{sample}:

$$CDF(\theta_{sample},\phi_{max}) = U_{[0,1],1}$$

so that

$$\frac{\phi_{max}}{2\pi}\left(1 - cos^2\theta_{sample}\right) = U_{[0,1],1},$$

and solving for θ_{sample}, we eventually find

$$\theta_{sample} = cos^{-1}\sqrt{1 - \frac{2\pi}{\phi_{max}}U_{[0,1],1}}.$$

Remember, here, that $\phi_{max} = 2\pi$. This reduces to $\theta_{sample} = cos^{-1}\sqrt{1 - U_{[0,1],1}}$.

Next, we must find ϕ_{sample} using the cross section of the CDF at θ_{sample}, that is, $CDF(\theta_{sample}, \phi)$. We also need to scale $U_{[0,1],2}$ as already described. See Figure 8-3 for reference. Now,

$$CDF\left(\theta_{sample}, \phi_{sample}\right) = \frac{\phi_{sample}}{2\pi}\left(1 - cos^2\theta_{sample}\right)$$

$$= U_{[0,1],2} \cdot CDF\left(\theta_{sample}, \phi_{max}\right)$$

$$= U_{[0,1],2} \cdot \frac{\phi_{max}}{2\pi}\left(1 - cos^2\theta_{sample}\right)$$

Solving for ϕ_{sample}, we first divide both sides of the equation by $(1 - cos^2\theta_{sample})$, getting

$$\frac{\phi_{sample}}{2\pi} = U_{[0,1],2} \cdot \frac{\phi_{max}}{2\pi}.$$

And finally, multiplying both sides by 2π, we have

$$\phi_{sample} = U_{[0,1],2} \cdot \phi_{max}.$$

In this context (that of the upper hemisphere domain of the solid angle measure), $\phi_{max} = 2\pi$, and thus, $\phi_{sample} = 2\pi U_{[0,1],2}$.

As an exercise, try repeating the normalization and sampling calculations, but this time use a PDF that fits the profile of $cos^n\theta$. As you encounter different BRDF functions, you may try incorporating additional factors into your PDF's profile for better importance sampling.[12]

Note   You will still need to convert to the Cartesian tangent space (i.e., shading) coordinates from local spherical coordinates, for use by a RenderMan global integrator.[13]

Ward Anisotropy

Until now, we've only discussed isotropic BRDFs, that is, those that do not use directions along the differential surface. With isotropic materials, no matter how the surface is rotated about its normal, the BRDF returns the same outgoing radiance, all else equal (i.e., the same light field).

Listing 8-2. Single specular lobe of the Ward (single-layer) BRDF. We use `RixBXLookupByName()` to automatically provide the `lpeId` field value (default) of the `RixLobeSampled` struct that allows us to set the type of lobe being sampled and evaluated. See the `GenerateSample()` and `Evaluate*()` routines of the `RixBxdf` for details on using these `struct`s for switching between evaluations of a given lobe passed by the global integrator. In the Marschner Wood Bxdf later in the chapter, we will discuss how to specify a second specular lobe for evaluation

```
void
WardBxdfPlugin::Synchronize(RixContext& ctx,
                RixSCSyncMsg syncMsg,
                RixParameterList const* parameterList)
```

---

[12] It will not always be possible to apply these methods analytically with closed-form solutions. Thus, other techniques have been developed and are described in: Philip Dutre, Kavita Bala, and Philippe Bekaert. *Advanced global illumination*. AK Peters/CRC Press, 2018. However, using a cosine distribution for analytic BRDF is used in many circumstances.

[13] These are (where r is set to one) $x = \sin(\theta)\cos(\phi)$, $y = \sin(\theta)\sin(\phi)$, and $z = \cos(\theta)$.

```
{
    PIXAR_ARGUSED(ctx);
    PIXAR_ARGUSED(syncMsg);
    PIXAR_ARGUSED(parameterList);

    if (syncMsg == k_RixSCRenderBegin)
    {
        s_specWardLobe =
            RixBXLookupLobeByName(ctx, false, false,
            true, false, WardBxdfPlugin::k_specWardLobeId,
            "Specular");

        s_specWardLobeTraits =
            RixBXLobeTraits(WardBxdfPlugin::s_specWardLobe);
    }
}
```

Anisotropic materials take into account surface directions. The simplest are BRDFs that use orthonormal directions relative to the surface in differential areas (local tangential coordinates).

The Ward anisotropic BRDF does exactly this. It is meant to model materials such as brushed metals (where macroscopic, but very small, grooves are not themselves an intrinsic material property, as modeled in the BRDF). Nonetheless, this BRDF exhibits highlights that are elongated perpendicular to the "groove" direction—really just a surface direction in the BRDF. Conceptually, one can think of these grooves as microscopic half cylinders raised from the surface and which produce a specular reflection when the light and viewing direction are in the plane perpendicular to the groove direction. See Figure 8-4.

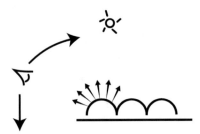

Figure 8-4. *When the eye and light source are in the plane perpendicular to the surface "grooves" (here running in the direction perpendicular to the paper), there is always a surface normal on the "groove" that is exactly halfway between the eye and light vector. Thus, a specular reflection occurs, and this is why highlights across the macro-surface are elongated*

The Ward model[14] (see Figure 8-5) uses a bivariate *Gaussian function* to map the angle **H** makes with the surface directions **u** and **v**, to the fraction of light reflected from the surface—for a given viewing and lighting angle to the surface normal **N**.

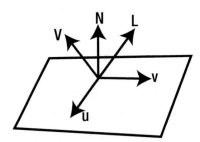

Figure 8-5. *Basic surface directions **u**, **v**, **N**, and **L**. **H** (not shown) is just the halfway vector between any two vectors spanning a plane. In pseudocode: normalize(**vector1** + **vector2**) = **H**. For the Ward Bxdf, the halfway vector is the vector halfway between Vn and Ln (indirect lighting direction)*

Note   We use the notation **N**, **L**, etc., and do not append an n to denote unit length. However, code in this chapter uses a suffix "n" to denote unit length. Assume the vectors discussed as follows are normalized (unit length).

---

[14] See:

Ward, Gregory J. "Measuring and modeling anisotropic reflection." *Proceedings of the 19th annual conference on computer graphics and interactive techniques*, 1992.

Guarnera, Giuseppe Claudio, et al. "BxDF material acquisition, representation, and rendering for VR and design." *SIGGRAPH Asia 2019 Courses*, 2019, 1–21.

The Ward BRDF computes the following angles using the unit-length **N**, **L**, **V**, **H**, **u**, and **v** vectors:

- $cos\,\theta_i$ – Cosine of the angle between **N** and **L**
- $cos\,\theta_r$ – Cosine of the angle between **N** and **V**
- $cos\,\theta_n$ – Cosine of the angle between **N** and **H**
- $cos\,\theta_u$ – Cosine of the angle between **H** and **u**
- $cos\,\theta_v$ – Cosine of the angle between **H** and **v**

The BRDF uses the following parameters:

- $u_{roughness}$ – "Roughness" in the **u** surface direction
- $v_{roughness}$ – "Roughness" in the **v** surface direction

Figure 8-6. *Ward Bxdf rendering showing "groove" direction switched between* ***u*** *and* ***v*** *by changing the Gaussian spread in the respective direction. The left rendering has* u_roughness *= 0.2 and* v_roughness *= 1.0. The rendering on the right has* u_roughness *= 1.0 and* v_roughness *= 0.2. The specular color was set to [0 1 1]. Light sources are two* PxrSphereLights *placed symmetrically and off center between the camera and the teapot. See the RIB included with the book's code sample*

Background on the Gaussian Curve

The general one-dimensional (univariate) Gaussian function is of the form

$$g(x) = A \cdot \exp\left(-\frac{(x-b)^2}{2c^2}\right).$$

And the two-dimensional (bivariate) Gaussian is

$$g(x,y) = A \cdot \exp\left(-\left(\frac{(x - x_o)^2}{2\sigma_X^2} + \frac{(y - y_o)^2}{2\sigma_Y^2}\right)\right).$$

A is the amplitude, x_o, y_o is the center, and σ_X, σ_Y are the x and y spreads of the "blob." These Gaussian curves are not normalized. We will use a normalized Gaussian, later in the chapter, when discussing the Marschner model.

The Ward Anisotropic BRDF

A version of the Ward model is

$$f_r = A \cdot \exp\left(-2 \frac{\left(\frac{\cos\theta_u}{u_{roughness}}\right)^2 + \left(\frac{\cos\theta_v}{v_{roughness}}\right)^2}{1 + \cos\theta_n}\right),$$

with A (amplitude) as

$$A = \frac{1}{\sqrt{\cos\theta_i \cos\theta_r}} \frac{1}{4\pi\sqrt{u_{roughness} v_{roughness}}}.$$

The amplitude depends on the Fresnel equations (not discussed here).[15] The amplitude does not contribute to the anisotropy of the Ward BRDF but serves to increase (or decrease) the overall amount of light reflected.

Visualizations of Ward BRDF specular lobes (in spherical coordinates) are shown in Figures 8-7 and 8-8, emphasizing the reflection distributions for the **u** and **v** principal surface directions and their relation to **L**.

---

[15] See the `RixFresnelDielectric()` in *RixShadingUtils.h*.

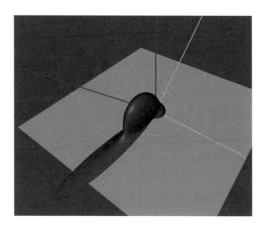

Figure 8-7. *Ward BRDF with **L** perpendicular to surface direction **u** for parameters $u_{roughness}$ = 0.387 and $v_{roughness}$ = 0.258. The lobe shows the distribution of the outgoing light over the extent of the **L** and **R** plane. Cyan direction is **L**, purple direction is **R**, and **u** is green. The **v** direction is red but covered by the lobe*

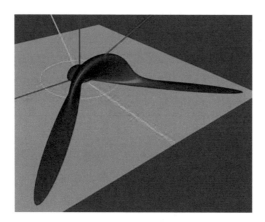

Figure 8-8. *Ward BRDF with incident **L** direction perpendicular to "groove" surface direction for $u_{roughness}$ = 1.0 and $v_{roughness}$ = 0.116. Notice the "cone" distribution along the "groove" (i.e., **u**). This is characteristic of specular fiber reflection (and is exhibited prominently in the Marschner wood material). Cyan direction is **L**, purple direction is **R**, and green is **u**. The **v** direction is red but covered by the lobe*

See Listing 8-3 for the C++ implementation of the BRDF using the aforementioned mathematical descriptions. Figure 8-9 describes the use of dPdu and dPdv. dPdu and dPdv are in the **u** and **v** unit vector surface directions mentioned earlier.

Note   It is best to normalize dPdu and dPdv if using these variables for the computation of an orthonormal basis with orthonormal directions **n**, **u**, and **v**.

Listing 8-3. Evaluation routine for the Ward BRDF. One of the main things to notice here is that RSL provides access to an `illuminance` loop using the built-in `Cl` (RSL light color) variable, per direct light. No such access is available in the path tracing framework for Bxdf. We must compare weights per color channel via `RtColorRGB` output (W in the code), which is the final calculation of the BRDF with the light dilution term to account for irradiance. The global integrator uses this with the value of Ln determined later. Ln is only the direction of the light sample (direct or indirect, depending on the global integrator used). The sample weights for the integral estimator of the rendering equation are outputs. Here, we are using the cosine distribution PDF discussed in a prior section of this chapter.[16] The output parameters are in boldface type

```
PRMAN_INLINE
void Ward::evaluateBRDF( // param table input
                    const RtColorRGB& specular,
                    const float u_roughness,
                    const float v_roughness,

                    // shading context input
                    const RtVector3 Nn,
                    const RtVector3 Ln,
                    const RtVector3 Vn,
                    const RtFloat3 dPdu,
                    const RtFloat3 dPdv,
```

---

[16] Be sure to refer to the RSL code included in this book's code repository to see the differences between the original RSL and the Bxdf C++ plugin. Most of the code from the RSL surface shader is in the plugin's "evaluation" routine.

```
                    // output:
                    RtColorRGB& W,
                    float& FPdf,
                    RtFloat& RPdf )
{
    RtVector3 H = Ln + Vn;
    H.Normalize();

    // calculate the parameters for the Ward Model
    float cos_theta_i = Nn.Dot(Ln);
    float cos_theta_r = Nn.Dot(Vn);
    float cos_theta_n = Nn.Dot(H);
    float cos_theta_u = H.Dot(dPdu);
    float cos_theta_v = H.Dot(dPdv);

    // calc. amplitude
    float A = ( 1.0 / sqrt( cos_theta_i * cos_theta_r ) )
        * ( 1.0 / ( 4 * F_PI * u_roughness * v_roughness ) );

    // calc. e part
    float num = pow( cos_theta_u / u_roughness, 2 ) +
                pow( cos_theta_v / v_roughness, 2 ) ;
    float den = 1 + cos_theta_n;
    float e_part = exp( -2 * num / den );

    float brdf = A * e_part;


    // Set outputs:
    W = specular * brdf
      * Nn.Dot(Vn); // radiance-to-irradiance

    // pdf values of Ln (FPdf) and Vn (RPdf)
    FPdf = Nn.Dot(Ln) * F_INVPI;
    RPdf = Nn.Dot(Vn) * F_INVPI;
}
```

The shading context (a RixShadingContext instance passed in from the global integrator) provides the u and v coordinates of the shade point P (also from RixShading Context) but does not provide orthonormal directions for P's local tangent space.

Originally in RSL, there were derivative operators Du() and Dv() that would take the partial derivative of P, providing the change of P's coordinates in world space relative to changes along the surface directions **u** and **v**. Now this is provided via the shading context's dPdu and dPdv variables instead. See Figure 8-9.

$$\vec{P} = \begin{bmatrix} x \\ y \\ z \end{bmatrix} \qquad \frac{\partial \vec{P}}{\partial u} = \begin{bmatrix} \frac{\partial x}{\partial u} \\ \frac{\partial y}{\partial u} \\ \frac{\partial z}{\partial u} \end{bmatrix} \qquad \frac{\partial \vec{P}}{\partial v} = \begin{bmatrix} \frac{\partial x}{\partial v} \\ \frac{\partial y}{\partial v} \\ \frac{\partial z}{\partial v} \end{bmatrix}$$

$$\qquad\qquad\qquad\qquad \uparrow \qquad\qquad\qquad\qquad\qquad\qquad \uparrow$$

$$\qquad\qquad\qquad\qquad Du(P) \qquad\qquad\qquad\qquad\qquad\qquad Dv(P)$$

Figure 8-9. *Changes of the surface coordinates in world space (xyz) along the orthonormal tangent space direction centered on P are provided by the shading context's dPdu and dPdv variables. There is a difference between u, v coordinates and **u, v** surface directions, which are calculated via the partial derivatives (and normalization). For comparison, RSL did not provide these values directly but used the Du() and Dv() built-in function (i.e., operators) instead. See the included Ward RSL and C++ code for this book*

Marschner Finished Wood

The Marschner model, as presented in its original paper, is treated as an intrinsic subsurface scattering distribution function with three basic lobes: a diffuse lobe that may be attenuated by a coating (finish) on wood and two specular lobes.

The first specular lobe is essentially the basic Phong specular highlight (Chapter 5). The Marschner model's unique aspect is the subsurface portion, which takes into account wood fibers running in some orientation within the surface of the wood material. Thus, we focus on this anisotropic specular lobe.[17]

---

[17] See the following paper for more detail: Marschner, Stephen R., et al. "Measuring and modeling the appearance of finished wood." *ACM SIGGRAPH 2005 Papers*, 2005, 727–734.

An example rendering of this Bxdf is shown in Figure 8-10, and the code listing for specifying its three lobes in our factory class is shown in Listing 8-4.

Figure 8-10. *Finished wood Bxdf for the maple data.[18] The original RSL allowed for selectively choosing the **u**, **v** extents into the fiber and diffuse color data. Here, we use the full data set over the intervals [0,1] for both **u** and **v**. This is due, in part, to reading texture data separately from the pattern plugin* PxrTexture. *Lookups are not done directly in the Bxdf plugin as with the original RSL. Very faintly, in the center of the polygon is a red Phong highlight, whereas highlights near the back left of the polygon are caused by fiber highlights. See the Marschner Bxdf plugin's test. rib included with the repository*

Listing 8-4. Synchronize() *from the Marschner wood Bxdf. This illustrates three lobes for evaluation by the* RixBxdf *object. We set* lpeId *directly using* RixBXLobeSampled(), *rather than* RixBXLookupLobeByName, *so the second specular lobe will be properly allocated and used by the global integrator*

```
void
FinishedWoodBxdfPlugin::Synchronize(RixContext& ctx,
 RixSCSyncMsg syncMsg, RixParameterList const* parameterList)
{
    PIXAR_ARGUSED(ctx);
    PIXAR_ARGUSED(syncMsg);
    PIXAR_ARGUSED(parameterList);
```

---

[18] See *www.cs.cornell.edu/~srm/publications/SG05-wood.html*

```
    if (syncMsg == k_RixSCRenderBegin)
    {
        s_diffFinishedWoodLobe = RixBXLookupLobeByName(ctx, false,
            false, true, false,
            FinishedWoodBxdfPlugin::k_diffFinishedWoodLobeId,
            "Diffuse");

        s_phongFinishedWoodLobe = RixBXLobeSampled( false
            , true
            , true
            , false
            , 0 // lpeId
            , FinishedWoodBxdfPlugin::k_phongFinishedWoodLobeId);

        s_fiberFinishedWoodLobe = RixBXLobeSampled( false
            , true
            , true
            , false
            , 1 // lpeId
            , FinishedWoodBxdfPlugin::k_fiberFinishedWoodLobeId);

        s_diffFinishedWoodLobeTraits  = RixBXLobeTraits(
                FinishedWoodBxdfPlugin::s_diffFinishedWoodLobe);
        s_phongFinishedWoodLobeTraits = RixBXLobeTraits(
                FinishedWoodBxdfPlugin::s_phongFinishedWoodLobe);
        s_fiberFinishedWoodLobeTraits = RixBXLobeTraits(
                FinishedWoodBxdfPlugin::s_fiberFinishedWoodLobe);
    }
}
```

Note   It is important to ensure that all intended lobes for your Bxdf are evaluated. Set the lobes using RixBXLobeSampled's constructor, using an explicit lped.

Much like the Ward model, the Marschner wood BSSDF is anisotropic. However, the anisotropy is caused by specular reflection from fibers (air tubes) within the cellulose of the wood, after refracting (bending) upon entering the surface finish. Reflection from the fiber is a regular anisotropic specular reflection occurring as a cone centered on the fiber direction.

Reflected specularity reemerges from the wood refracted again at the surface interface. The subsurface geometry is shown in Figure 8-11. The cone of reflected specular rays is in the angle ψ_i (angle of inclination to the fiber normal) as labeled in the figure.

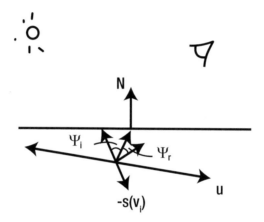

Figure 8-11. *The top-surface and subsurface geometry (with emphasis) in the Marschner wood model. $s(v_i)$ is the refracted incident vector (incident refracted direction calculated by* RixFresnelDielectric()*) from the surface in world coordinates. ψ_i and ψ_r are the angles of inclination of the incident and reflected rays relative to the subsurface direction **u**. Note that **u**, as it is used here, is not a surface direction—as it was in the Ward model—but the fiber direction within the volume of the material (nomenclature used from Marschner's original paper). A halfway vector is shown (unlabelled) between the incident and reflected vectors*

Listing 8-5 shows the computation of the dilution and refracted light directions by the wood's finish.

Listing 8-5. computeSubSurf() from FinishedWood RixBxdf. This member function computes the refracted ray directions mentioned in Figure 8-11 and the attenuation of incident irradiance used by the diffuse and Phong specular lobe evaluations (not shown but included in the book's code repository)

```
PRMAN_INLINE
void FinishedWood::computeSubSurf(
    const RtNormal3 Nn, const RtVector3 Ln,
    const RtVector3 Vn, const float eta,

    // output:
    RtVector3& ssInDir, RtVector3& ssOutDir,
    RtFloat& ssAtten,RtFloat& ssAttenOut)
{
    RtFloat Kr;
    RtVector3 Rdir;

    // If there is a clear overcoat, calculate refraction
    // direction and attenuation.
    RixFresnelDielectric( Vn, Nn, 1.0 / eta,
                &Kr, &Rdir, &ssOutDir );

    // Use (1-Kr) rather than Kt, because we are dealing with
    // power, not radiance.
    ssAtten = 1 - Kr;

    // Refract at smooth surface
    RixFresnelDielectric( Ln, Nn, 1.0 / eta,
                &Kr, &Rdir, &ssInDir );
    // Use (1-Kr) rather than Kt, because we are dealing with
    // power, not radiance.
    ssAttenOut = 1 - Kr;
}
```

Listing 8-6 shows the fiber reflection portion (a specular lobe) of the Bxdf. Mathematically, this is modeled by the following anisotropic BRDF. f_f is only the fiber portion of the full BSSDF f_r.[19]

f_f is composed of a Guassian function, like the Ward BRDF. $g(\sigma, x)$ is the normalized Gaussian (integrates to unity) with mean at zero. x designates a parameter from the domain of $g(\sigma, x)$. f_f is

$$f_f = k_f \frac{g(\beta, \psi_h)}{cos^2\left(\dfrac{\psi_d}{2}\right)}.$$

Its parameter descriptions are as follows:

- k_f – Contribution per color channel (a vector of weights) to the outgoing fiber reflection (analogous to the coefficient k_d or k_s for the diffuse and Phong specular lobes).

- ψ_d – The difference between the two inclination angles, that is, $\psi_r - \psi_i$. The larger the inclination difference between the subsurface incident ray and subsurface reflected ray, as measured from the fiber axis normal, the less intense the highlight—all else equal.[20]

- ψ_h – The halfway inclination measurement, that is, $\psi_r + \psi_i$. Because both ψ_r and ψ_i are signed, they represent rotations away from the fiber normal, but in opposite directions. For instance, if both are equal angles from the fiber normal, then the normal itself is the halfway between with an inclination of zero. For perfectly reflected rays, the highlight is greatest, all else equal, that is, when not considering the effect of ψ_d.

- β – The "spread" of $g(\sigma, x)$.

---

[19] Refer to this book's code and Marschner's paper mentioned previously.

[20] The squared cosine term in the denominator of the fiber lobe BRDF is described by Marschner as the "geometry factor for specular reflection into a cone." For a flat surface, this is just the unsquared cosine term. Note how similar this is to the Phong specular lobe/BRDF, but over a fiber and not a flat surface. As the BRDF exhibits perfect specularity, it must go to infinity when ψ_d is zero.

The implementation of the fiber lobe evaluation is shown in Listing 8-6. There you can also see how the angles of subsurface rays ψ_r and ψ_i are calculated. The refraction is handled in computeSubSurf() from Listing 8-5, which uses the utility RixFresnelDielectric().

Note   We continue to use the cosine distribution for all of our light samples. You may want to experiment with a different sampling function for this lobe, one that includes some of the factors of f_f.

Listing 8-6. evaluateFiberLobe() of FinishedWood RixBxdf. Some of the comments are from Steve Westin's original implementation in RSL. The RSL code is included in the book's repository along with the C++ Bxdf plugin. The call to computeSubSurf() is shown in boldface, along with the final output parameter assignments

```
PRMAN_INLINE
void FinishedWood::evaluateFiberLobe(
 const RtNormal3 Nn, const RtVector3 Ln, const RtVector3 Vn,
 const RtFloat3 dPdu, const RtFloat3 dPdv, const RtFloat u,
 const RtFloat v,

 // parameter table inputs:
 const float eta, const RtVector3 fiberAxis,const float beta,
 const RtColorRGB& fiberColor, const RtColorRGB Ks,

 // outputs:
 RtColorRGB& W, float& FPdf, RtFloat& RPdf)
{
    PIXAR_ARGUSED(dPdv);
    PIXAR_ARGUSED(u);
    PIXAR_ARGUSED(v);
```

```
// Calculate orthonormal basis around normal and u dirs
RtNormal3 local_z =
    RixGetForwardFacingNormal(Vn, Nn); // Surface normal
                                       // in "world" space
RtVector3 local_x = dPdu; // Unit vector in "u" dir
RtVector3 local_y = local_z.Cross(local_x); // Unit vector
                                            // in "v" dir

// Attenuation from going through the smooth interface twice
RtFloat ssAtten = 0.0f;
RtFloat& ref_ssAtten = ssAtten;
RtFloat ssAttenOut = 0.0f;
RtFloat& ref_ssAttenOut = ssAttenOut;
RtVector3 ssInDir = RtVector3(0.0f);
RtVector3& ref_ssInDir = ssInDir; // Light vector,
                                  // possibly refracted
RtVector3 ssOutDir = RtVector3(0.0f);
RtVector3& ref_ssOutDir = ssOutDir; // Reflected light
                                    // dir ("eye") vector

computeSubSurf(local_z, Ln, Vn, eta, ref_ssInDir,
        ref_ssOutDir, ref_ssAtten, ref_ssAttenOut);

RtFloat ssFactor =  RixMax( 0.0f, -1.0f
                    * ssInDir.Dot( local_z ) )
                    * ssAtten * ssAttenOut;

// Transform to local coord. sys.
// modified from tex lookup
RtVector3 axis =   ( fiberAxis[0] * 2 - 1.0 ) * local_x
                 - ( fiberAxis[1] * 2 - 1.0 ) * local_y
                 + ( fiberAxis[2] * 2 - 1.0 ) * local_z;
axis.Normalize();

RtFloat thOutPrime = asin ( ssOutDir.Dot( axis ) );
RtFloat thInPrime  = asin ( -ssInDir.Dot( axis ) );

RtFloat halfAngle = thOutPrime + thInPrime;
```

```
    RtFloat diffAngle = thOutPrime - thInPrime;

    RtFloat tx_beta = beta;
    RtColorRGB highlight = fiberColor * 20; // modified from
                                            // texture lookup

    // Compute value of Gaussian at this angle
    RtFloat cosIncline = cos( diffAngle / 2 );
    RtFloat geometryFactor = 1 / pow ( cosIncline, 2 );

    RtFloat fiberFactor =
        tx_beta * geometryFactor
      * exp ( -pow( halfAngle / tx_beta, 2 ) / 2 ) / SQRT_2PI;

    // Set OUTPUTs:
    // Add in fiber highlight, also attenuated.
    W = fiberFactor * highlight * ssFactor;

    // cosine distribution pdf values
    FPdf = Nn.Dot(Ln) * F_INVPI;
    RPdf = Nn.Dot(Vn) * F_INVPI;

}
```

Summary

In this chapter, we discussed anisotropic Bxdf, that is, those whose orientation about their surface normal changes the light reflection distribution. We also described calculations for determining a PDF (normalization) and for using the inverse bivariate CDF to draw samples using the PDF's density distribution.

Some intrinsic BxDF might be treated using separate materials and accounting for transmission between them. However, this was all handled as part of the "fiber" lobe evaluation in the original Marschner finished wood BSSDF.

Conclusions

This book has been dedicated to writing Bxdf plugins, that is, those that program to the interface of the `RixBxdf` and `RixShadingPlugin` classes of the `Rix` API. This represents a deviation from classic RSL and surface shader domains.

With surface shaders, one would have both explicit knowledge of light contributions (`Cl`) in the `illuminance` loop and be able to write out patterns (procedural surface colors).

As noted, Bxdf plugins only allow for handling light interaction with materials and take varying output from "pattern" plugins instead as input. There is, however, the option of using Open Shading Language (OSL) code for patterns, providing a more traditional RSL experience within modern RenderMan.[1]

We did not cover transmission and opacity, that is, the use of the following pairs:

- `RixShadingPlugin::BeginTransmission()`, `RixShadingPlugin::End Transmission()`

- `RixShadingPlugin::BeginOpacity()`, `RixShadingPlugin::End Opacity()`

These were omitted in the interest of providing an introduction to writing Bxdf plugins without the added complexity (unfortunately not the case with some of the official Pixar examples, even `PxrDiffuse`).

Now that you have a foundation in Bxdf plugin architecture, try rewriting the Marschner wood shader of this chapter using transmission, instead of treating the BSSDF as a single intrinsic Bxdf. The official Pixar documentation discusses transmission and opacity in detail.

---

[1] For an intro to using OSL with Blender Cycles (which provides some nice examples of OSL procedural patterns), see *Open Shading Language for Blender: A Practical Primer, Michel Anders, ISBN: 9781301681471,* `www.smashwords.com/books/view/368598`

© Brad E. Hollister 2023
B. E. Hollister, *Essential Guide to RenderMan® Shading Plugin Development*,
https://doi.org/10.1007/978-1-4842-9392-8

Index

A

Application programming interface (API)
    C programming, 12, 13
    Python script, 13, 14
    Ri documentation, 13
    Rix shader plugins, 57–68

B

Bidirectional reflectance distribution
        function (BRDF), 42
    path tracing, 42
    rendering equation, 44
    ward anisotropic, 122–126
Bidirectional scattering distribution
        functions (BxDF), 1
    canonical sampling, 71
    contributions (Cl), 135
    definitions, 42
    development environment, 97
        debugging tools, 99
        PxrDebugShadingContext,
          104, 105
        PxrValidateBxdf, 102–104
        renderman.ini file, 101
        Vim/Emacs, 98
        VS Code extensions, 101, 102
        Windows, 99
        Xcode/Visual Studio, 97
    PDFs development, 107

radiometry, 33
Rix API, 57
Bidirectional subsurface scattering
        function (BSSD), 107

C

C++ programming language
    Args file, 32
    Bxdf plugin, 28, 32
    compilation, 28
    dynamic/static linking, 31
    Makefile, 28–30
    object-oriented methodologies, 27
    plugin folder, 31, 32
    reserved words, 24–27
    server files, 31
    shader plugins, 24
    shared objects, 31
    targets, 30
Canonical scattering regimes
    code organization, 72, 73
    diffuse reflection model
        evaluateBRDF(), 91
        EvaluateSample(), 87
        factory class, 82, 83
        GenerateSample(), 85, 87
        Lambertian spherical plot, 80–82
        PDF selection/sampling, 89–92
        RixBxdf object, 84–89
        RixBXLookupLobeByName(), 83

© Brad E. Hollister 2023
B. E. Hollister, *Essential Guide to RenderMan® Shading Plugin Development*,
https://doi.org/10.1007/978-1-4842-9392-8

V

W, X, Y, Z

Printed in the United States
by Baker & Taylor Publisher Services